Geograpny Today

for ages 10–11

Andrew Brodie

Published 2008 by A&C Black Publishers Limited
38 Soho Square, London W1D 3HB
www.acblack.com

ISBN 9781408104583

Copyright © A&C Black Publishers Limited

Written by Andrew Brodie and Judy Richardson
Illustration by Mike Phillips/Beehive Illustration
Maps by Tony Randall
Photographs by Andrew Brodie and Judy Richardson
Page layout by Bob Vickers

A CIP record for this publication is available from the British Library.

All rights reserved. This book may be photocopied, for use in the educational establishment for which it was purchased, but may not be reproduced in any other form or by any means - graphic, electronic, or mechanical, including photocopying, recording, taping or information storage or retrieval systems - without the prior permission in writing of the publishers.

Printed by Martin's the Printers, Berwick-upon-Tweed

This book is produced using paper that is made from wood grown in managed, sustainable forests. It is natural, renewable and recyclable. The logging and manufacturing processes conform to the environmental regulations of the country of origin.

To see our full range of titles visit www.acblack.com

CONTENTS

	Page number
INTRODUCTION	4
RECORD SHEET	8
MAPS – THE WORLD, EUROPE AND THE UNITED KINGDOM	9
USING ORDNANCE SURVEY MAPS	23
LOCAL MAPS	28
THE POWER OF THE WIND	33
RIVERS	39
MOUNTAINS	54
EXTENSION ACTIVITY	64

INTRODUCTION

The *Geography Today* series provides ample opportunities to make geography the most exciting subject on the curriculum. Based on the demands of the National Curriculum, the contents of the books reflect the need to put fun and enjoyment back into geography by ensuring that people and places are at the heart of the subject.

Never have we been more aware of global issues. Geography provides the key to helping children understand the world, its diverse environments and the roles and impacts that people create. Throughout the *Geography Today* series, children will develop their awareness of the world while building an enthusiasm for the subject of geography. At Year 6 pupils will examine major physical features: rivers and mountains.

Each book in the series consists of differentiated worksheets of fun classroom activities and fieldwork exercises. The accompanying CD-ROM contains copies of all worksheets in PDF format, together with photographs and maps to display on the whiteboard, offering many possibilities for discussion and interaction.

Much of the work should be completed as speaking, listening and visual activities. Maps and photographs on the CD-ROM offer many possibilities for discussion and interaction. In particular, pupils will be encouraged to 'use a range of oral techniques to present persuasive arguments and engaging narratives' (Literacy Framework Year Six Speaking) and to 'make notes when listening for a sustained period' (Literacy Framework Year Six Listening).

QCA guidance for geography suggests the possible use of two units specifically for Year Six and other units for more than one age-group:

- Investigating Rivers
- The Mountain Environment
- Investigating Coasts (Y5–Y6)
- What's in the news? (Y3–Y6)
- Connecting ourselves to the world (Y3–Y6)
- Passport to the world (Y1–Y6)
- Geography and numbers (Y1–Y6)

Geography Today provides support for schools following the QCA guidance as the resources can be slotted in to current teaching programmes. However some schools may prefer to use our materials independently of the QCA guidance, confident in the knowledge that they are meeting the requirements of the National Curriculum.

The National Curriculum for Key Stage Two divides geography into seven programmes of study:

1. Geographical enquiry and skills 1, which considers asking geographical questions; collecting and recording evidence; analysing evidence and drawing conclusions; identifying and explaining different views that people, including themselves, hold about topical geographical issues; communicating in ways appropriate to the task and audience.

2. Geographical enquiry and skills 2, which includes using geographical vocabulary; using fieldwork techniques and instruments; using globes, maps and plans; using secondary sources of information, including aerial photographs; drawing plans and maps at a range of scales; using ICT to help in geographical investigations; using decision-making skills.

3. Knowledge and understanding of places, including identifying and describing what places are like; the locations of places and environments they study and other significant places and environments; describing where places are; explaining why places are like they are; identifying how and why places change and how they may change in the future; describing and explaining how and why places are similar to and different from other places in the same country and elsewhere in the world.

4. Knowledge and understanding of patterns and processes, including recognising and explaining patterns made by individual physical and human features in the environment; recognising some physical and human processes and explaining how these can cause changes in places and environments.

5. Knowledge and understanding of environmental change and sustainable development, including recognising how people can improve the environment or damage it, and how decisions about places and environments affect the future quality of people's lives; recognising how and why people may seek to manage environments sustainably, and to identify opportunities for their own involvement.

6. Breadth of study through the study of two localities, one in the United Kingdom and one in a country that is less economically developed, and three themes:

    - water and its effects on landscapes and people, including the physical features of rivers or coasts, and the processes of erosion and deposition that affect them;

    - how settlements differ and change, including why they differ in size and character, and an issue arising from changes in land use;

    - an environmental issue, caused by change in an environment, and attempts to manage the environment sustainably.

7. Breadth of study – studying at a range of scales, local, regional and national; studying a range of places and environments in different parts of the world, including the UK and the EU; carrying out fieldwork investigations outside the classroom.

Places and environments listed in the National Curriculum as required for locational knowledge:

British Isles:
The two largest islands of the British Isles: Great Britain, Ireland.
The two countries: United Kingdom, the Republic of Ireland.
Capitals: Belfast, Cardiff, Dublin, Edinburgh, London.
Mountain areas: Cambrians, Grampians, Lake District, Pennines.
Longest rivers in UK: Severn, Thames, Trent.
Seas around UK: English Channel, Irish Sea, North Sea.

Europe:
Three EU countries with highest populations and their capitals: France, Germany, Italy; Paris, Berlin, Rome.
Three EU countries with largest areas and their capitals: France, Spain, Sweden; Paris, Madrid, Stockholm.
Largest mountain range: Alps
Longest river in countries listed above: Rhine
Largest seas: Mediterranean, North Sea.

World:
Continents: Africa, Asia, Europe, North America, Oceania, South America, Antarctica.
Largest city in each continent: Lagos, Tokyo, Paris, New York, Sydney, Sao Paulo.
Six countries with highest populations: Brazil, China, India, Indonesia, Russia, USA.
Six countries with largest areas: Australia, Brazil, Canada, China, Russia, USA.
Areas of family origin of the main minority ethnic groups in UK: Bangladesh, Caribbean, India, Pakistan, Republic of Ireland.
Largest mountain ranges on basis of height and extent: Andes, Himalayas, Rocky Mountains.
Three longest rivers: Amazon, Mississippi, Nile.
Largest desert: Sahara.
Oceans: Arctic, Atlantic, Indian, Pacific.
Canals linking seas/oceans: Panama, Suez.
North Pole, South Pole, Equator, Tropics, Prime Meridian.

Geography offers a multitude of opportunities for cross-curricular work. *Geography Today* gives a range of experiences in the following areas:

- Speaking and Listening, when considering all the worksheets, photographs and presentations.
- Reading, when sharing information on paper and on screen.
- Writing, when responding to questions and when making statements.
- Number, when counting people or things in surveys, when counting houses, shops, etc.
- Shape and DT, when constructing models.
- Art and Science, when making close observations in fieldwork.
- Religious Education, when sensing the awe and wonder of the world.
- ICT, when working interactively.
- History, when considering the local area and the changes that are taking place.

Geography Today 10–11

The book is divided into six units. Each unit contains worksheets that are suitable for all pupils and some have differentiated worksheets that are targeted at **three different levels**:

 sheets marked with a cat are the least demanding,

 sheets marked with a dog are suitable for most pupils,

 sheets marked with a rabbit are more difficult.

You may wish to use all three worksheets with some pupils, but to use just one or two for others. Key vocabulary used in a unit is provided at the end of each unit. Where relevant, a unit will have an accompanying CD-ROM presentation, providing a focus for discussion and serving as an introduction to the worksheets. Where individual worksheets are linked to the CD-ROM this symbol will be displayed in the teachers' notes.

Unit 1: Maps – The World, Europe and the United Kingdom
This unit focuses on developing awareness of places in the world. The CD-ROM photographs lead pupils from examining the map of the whole world, through considering a map of Europe, to looking closely at the UK. The worksheets are designed to strengthen pupils' knowledge of key locations on the maps, ensuring that they are aware of all the places listed in the National Curriculum. Pupils learn map reference skills and apply these in identifying the key locations.

Unit 2: Using Ordnance Survey maps
This unit focuses on gaining an understanding of how to use local maps, such as Ordnance Survey maps and recognise the Ordnance Survey symbols. The CD-ROM presentation introduces map symbols and the worksheets use map symbols and grid references in relation to a map of a small seaside area.

Unit 3: Local maps
This unit focuses on gaining an understanding of how to use local maps, such as Ordnance Survey maps. The CD-ROM presentation provides revision of points of the compass and further work on grid references, introducing six figure grid references, as well as work on scale. The worksheets use grid references, points of the compass and scale in relation to a map of a small seaside town.

Unit 4: The Power of the Wind
This unit provides an opportunity for the pupils to debate a potentially contentious issue – the construction of a wind farm in the local area. There is an accompanying CD-ROM presentation.

Unit 5: Rivers
This unit encourages pupils to look more closely at rivers in this country and abroad. There is an extended CD-ROM presentation and worksheet activities to stimulate discussion and introduce pupils to some of the special terminology we might use in relation to rivers. Pupils consider the importance of rivers, conduct research on a local river and learn about famous rivers.

Unit 6: Mountains
This unit is centred around the speaking and listening activity prompted by the CD-ROM presentation. Pupils are encouraged to observe carefully and identify features of mountain environments around the world. They are also encouraged to consider the types of human activity in various mountain environments. The worksheets provide opportunities for investigations using the internet or other resources. At the end of this unit there is an extension activity for pupils to use some of the skills and knowledge they have acquired throughout the Geography Today series. Pupils choose a country of their choice, find out about it, and prepare a presentation.

RECORD SHEET

Name **Sophia (age 10)**

National Curriculum Level 3

I can show my knowledge in studies at a local scale.

I can show my skills in studies at a local scale.

I can show my understanding in studies at a local scale.

I can describe and compare physical features of different localities and offer explanations for the location of some of those features.

I can describe and compare human features of different localities and offer explanations for the location of some of those features.

I am aware that different places may have both similar and different characteristics.

I offer reasons for some of my observations and for my views and judgements about places and environments.

I recognise how people seek to improve and sustain environments.

I can use skills and sources of evidence to respond to a range of geographical questions.

I am beginning to use appropriate vocabulary to communicate my findings.

National Curriculum Level 4

I can show my knowledge, skills and understanding in studies of a range of places and environments at more than one scale and in different parts of the world.

I am beginning to recognise and describe geographical patterns.

I am beginning to appreciate the importance of wider geographical location in understanding places.

I can recognise and describe physical processes.

I can recognise and describe human processes.

I am beginning to understand how physical and human processes can change the features of places and how these changes affect the lives and activities of people living there.

I understand how people can both improve and damage the environment.

I can explain my views and the views of other people about an environmental change.

I can suggest suitable geographical questions to help me to investigate places and environments.

I can use a range of geographical skills to help me to investigate places and environments.

I use primary and secondary sources of evidence in investigations.

I can communicate my findings using appropriate vocabulary.

National Curriculum Level 5

I can show my knowledge, skills and understanding in studies of a range of places and environments at more than one scale and in different parts of the world.

I can describe geographical patterns and physical and human processes.

I am beginning to explain geographical patterns and physical and human processes.

I can describe how these processes can lead to similarities and differences in the environments of different places and in the lives of people who live there.

I can recognise some of the links and relationships that make places dependent on each other.

I can suggest explanations for the ways in which human activities cause changes to the environment and the different views people hold about them.

I recognise how people try to manage environments sustainably.

I explain my own views and I am beginning to suggest relevant geographical questions and issues.

I select and use appropriate skills and ways of presenting information to help me investigate places and environments.

I select information and sources of evidence.

I suggest plausible conclusions to my investigations.

I present my findings both graphically and in writing.

MAPS – THE WORLD, EUROPE AND THE UNITED KINGDOM

Contents

This unit focuses on developing awareness of places in the world. The CD-ROM photographs lead pupils from examining the map of the whole world, through considering a map of Europe, to looking closely at the United Kingdom. The worksheets are designed to strengthen pupils' knowledge regarding key locations on the maps, ensuring that they are aware of all the places listed in the National Curriculum. Pupils learn map reference skills and apply these in identifying the key locations.

This unit features:
- CD-ROM: MAPS 1–4
- Worksheets 1–8
- Vocabulary sheets 1–3

Useful resources

- atlas of the World
- globe

Learning objectives

- asking geographical questions
- using appropriate geographical vocabulary
- using atlases and globes, and maps and plans at a range of scales
- using secondary sources of information
- drawing maps and plans at a range of scales
- identifying and describing what places are like
- locating and describing where places are
- recognising how places fit within a wider geographical context
- recognising physical and human features in the environment

The worksheets

Worksheet 1: Can I use map references on a world map?
Worksheet 2: World Map
Worksheet 3: Can I show physical features on a world map?
Worksheet 4: World Map
Worksheet 5: Can I use map references on a map of Europe?
Worksheet 6: Map of Europe
Worksheet 7: Can I use map references on a map of the British Isles?
Worksheet 8: Map of British Isles

The vocabulary sheets

The sheets can also be photocopied then made into flashcards, which can be used for both geography and literacy. You may wish to ask the pupils to sort them into categories such as continents, oceans, seas, countries, capital cities, rivers, mountains, deserts, etc.

The CD-ROM

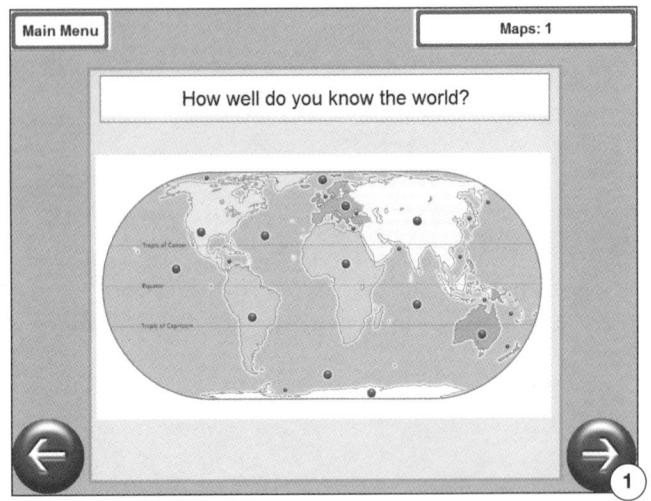

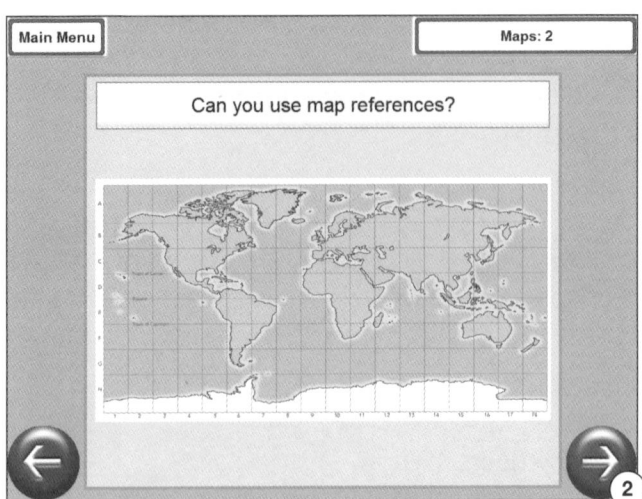

This interactive map provides an opportunity to revise previous learning about the names of the continents and the oceans. By moving over the red dots names of the continents and seas and oceans of the world will appear. Point out that Antarctica appears like a ribbon along the bottom of the map because the map is a flat representation of a sphere – compare the map to a globe, pointing out Antarctica on both. Discuss the Arctic – unlike Antarctica the Arctic consists largely of a frozen ocean rather than any land mass and is therefore not a continent. Point out the Equator to the pupils and explain that the area to the north of the Equator is called the northern hemisphere and the area to the south is called the southern hemisphere. Do the children understand the term 'hemisphere' or can they work out that it means half a sphere? Explain that the Equator is an imaginary line – it is not drawn on the Earth's surface, except in a few places where humans have drawn it to show to tourists! Show the pupils the tropics – the line called the Tropic of Cancer to the north of the Equator and the Tropic of Capricorn to the south. Can the children think of ideas to remember which is which? Do they know what the tropic lines show? Only between the two tropic lines can the sun be directly overhead. On 21st June each year the sun is directly over the Tropic of Cancer and on 21st December each year the sun is directly over the Tropic of Capricorn. On 21st March and 21st September it is directly above the Equator.

Can the children identify each of the continents and the major oceans? You might like to give the pupils some quiz-type questions, encouraging them to identify particular continents, oceans or seas. The clues below relate to Africa, Indian Ocean, South America, Arctic Ocean. When the pupils answer the questions correctly move over the appropriate red dot to label the area that has been identified.

I am thinking of a continent. It is in both the northern and the southern hemisphere. The River Nile flows through it. What continent am I thinking of?

I am thinking of an ocean. It is between Africa and Australia. What ocean am I thinking of?

I am thinking of a continent. It is mainly in the southern hemisphere but partly in the northern hemisphere. The River Amazon flows through it. What continent am I thinking of?

I am thinking of an ocean. It is situated at the most northerly part of the world. Much of it is frozen but people are now worried that the ice is melting. What ocean am I thinking of?

The next slide shows the map of the world again but this time some specific countries are highlighted.

Ask the children if they can spot the difference between this map and the previous one. Hopefully they will be able to identify the grid that is now shown. Discuss a globe with the children showing them the lines that appear vertically – the lines of longitude – and the lines that appear horizontally – the Equator, the Tropics and the lines of latitude. Can the children see how the lines of the grid split the map into sections? Can they see the numbers given for each vertical section and the capital letters for each horizontal section?

Can they use the letters to identify individual blocks on the map? Ask them to identify the block in which most of the United Kingdom appears. Point out that one line of longitude passes through the United Kingdom, specifically through Greenwich in London – this line is called the prime meridian and is the internationally agreed line of 0 degrees and every other line of longitude relates to this. They should find that the UK appears in block 9B – note that some atlases follow the convention of representing the position North-South first, then the position West-East second and therefore the block would be identified by the capital letter before the number. This contrasts with the mathematical convention of representing the x-coordinate before the y-coordinate, but also more significantly contrasts with the convention of representing 'Eastings' before 'Northings', as on Ordnance Survey maps. You could discuss other places on the map, identifying their positions by the grid references.

The CD-ROM continued

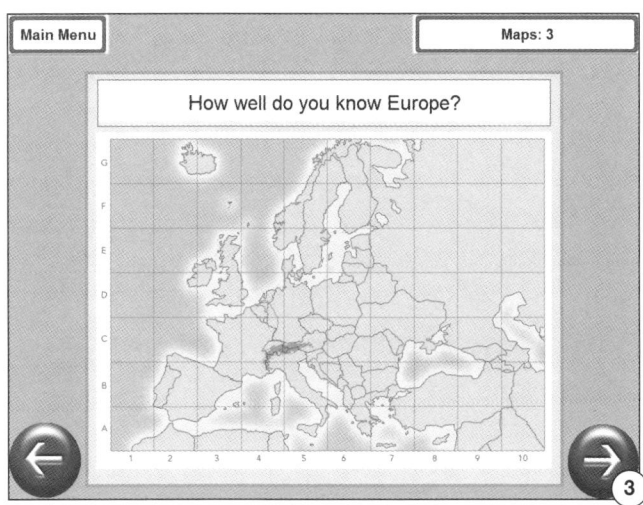

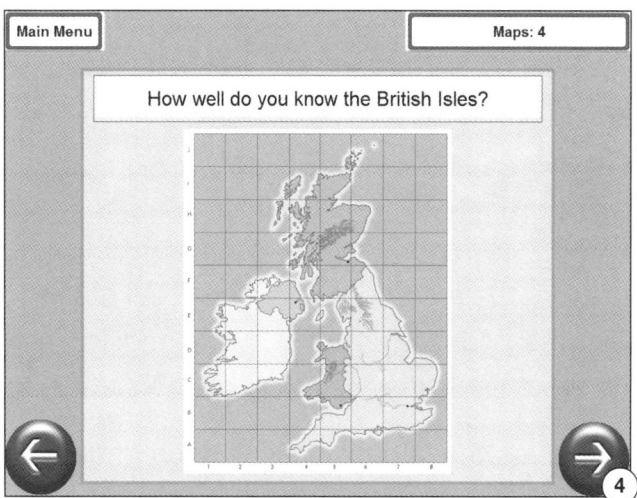

Can the children identify some of the countries? The National Curriculum states that they should know the three countries with the largest areas and their capital cities – France, Spain and Sweden – and the three countries with the highest populations and their capital cities – France, Germany and Italy. Our map shows all of the countries and you could encourage the children to know the positions of the major countries and of any countries with which the class may have connections. Again, you may like to involve the pupils in some quiz questions, such as those below – the pupils could also create their own quiz questions to share with the class.

I am thinking of a country in the northern part of Europe. It is one of the three countries with the greatest land area in Europe. Its capital is Stockholm. What country am I thinking of?

I am thinking of a country that is east of Germany. It is south of the Baltic Sea. Its capital is Warsaw. What country am I thinking of?

I am thinking of a country that is mainly in grid square 6B. What country am I thinking of?

I am thinking of a sea that is in grid square 4E. What sea am I thinking of?

Can the children identify the countries? *Do you know that the British Isles consist of over six thousand islands, the largest of which is Great Britain and the second largest is Ireland?* Do they understand that there are two countries, the United Kingdom and the Republic of Ireland, but that the UK is split into Northern Ireland, Scotland, Wales and England? Can they identify the capital cities, Dublin, Belfast, Edinburgh, Cardiff, London?

Discuss the physical features that are shown on the map: the River Severn, River Thames, River Trent; the Cambrian Mountains, the Grampian Mountains, the Lake District, the Pennines. Explain that there are lots of rivers and mountains in the British Isles and that just some of them are shown on the map.

Can the pupils identify your own area? They could point to where they think it is on the map or they could suggest a grid reference using the numbers and letters shown. They could use an atlas to check if they are correct.

You may like to ask the children some quiz questions:

Can you identify a river that has its source in Wales then flows through England into the Bristol Channel?

What mountain range is sometimes known as the backbone of England?

What river flows through London?

The highest mountain in the UK is called Ben Nevis. What mountain range is it in?

Maps — Worksheet 1

Can I use map references on a world map

Name __Sophia__ Date __4/11/22__

Look at the map on Worksheet 2. All of the following cities are marked on the map. Use the grid references shown alongside each city's name to find its correct position on the map. Write the name of each city in the correct place.

These are the largest cities in each of the continents:

~~Lagos 10D~~   ~~Tokyo 16C~~   ~~Paris 10B~~   ~~New York 6C~~   ~~Sydney 17F~~   Sao Paulo 7F

All of the following countries are shaded on the map. Use the grid references shown alongside each country's name to find its correct position on the map – note that some countries are so big that they extend beyond the block shown by the grid reference. Colour the whole of each country and write its name in the correct place.

These are the countries with the six highest populations in the world:

Brazil 7E   China 15C   India 13D   Indonesia 15E   Russia 13B   USA 4C

Two more countries are also shaded on the map. Use the grid references shown alongside each country's name to find its correct position on the map. Colour the whole of each country and write its name in the correct place.

These are the countries with the six highest land areas in the world:

Australia 16F   Brazil 7E   **Canada 4B**   China 15C   Russia 13B   USA 4C

Teachers' notes This worksheet needs to be used in conjunction with Worksheet 2 which shows a map of the world and a grid referencing system. Pupils use the grid references to find cities and countries while learning some of the key geographical facts from the National Curriculum Programmes of Study.

Maps Worksheet 2

Map of the world

Name Sophia   Date 4/11/22

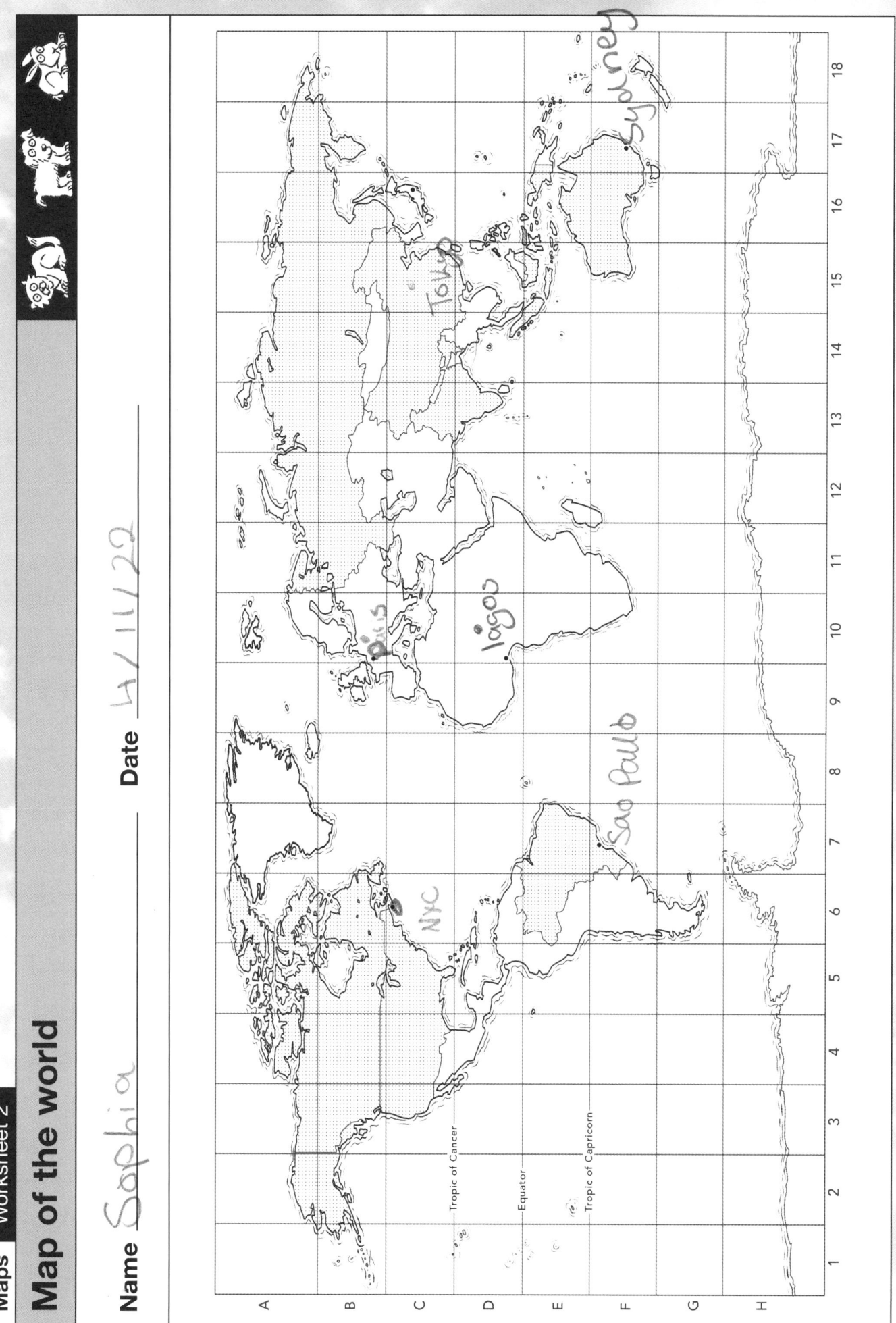

Teachers' notes This worksheet needs to be used in conjunction with Worksheet 1 which gives the grid references to find cities and countries. Please note that some countries extend beyond the block given by the grid reference.

Maps Worksheet 3

Can I show physical features on a world map?

Name _____ Date _____

Look at the map on Worksheet 4. All of the following mountains or mountain ranges are marked on the map. Use the grid references shown alongside each mountain range's name to find its correct position on the map. Write the name of each mountain or mountain range in the correct place.

Andes 6F   Alps 10B   Atlas Mountains 9C
Himalayas 13C   Kilimanjaro 11E   Rocky Mountains 4C

What is the name of the highest mountain in the world?

_____

Use the internet or an encyclopedia or atlas to find out how tall it is.

_____

There are lots of deserts in the world and some of them are marked on the map. The biggest desert is the Sahara Desert. Use the grid references shown alongside each desert's name to find its correct position on the map. Write the name of each desert in the correct place.

Sahara 10D   Kalahari Desert 10E   Gobi Desert 14C   Great Victoria Desert 16F

All of the following rivers are marked on the map. Use the grid references shown alongside each river's name to find its correct position on the map. Write the name of each river in the correct place.

Amazon 6E   Mississippi 5C   Nile 11D

Mountains, deserts and rivers are all physical features. Human features are things that have been created by people, such as buildings and canals. Two very important canals are shown on the map. Why do you think that these canals are so important?

Panama Canal 5D   Suez Canal 11C

Teachers' notes This worksheet needs to be used in conjunction with Worksheet 4, which shows a map of the world and a grid referencing system. Pupils use the grid references to find certain mountains, deserts and rivers while learning some of the key geographical facts from the National Curriculum Programmes of Study. Discuss the importance of the two canals encouraging pupils to realise that they link major seas or oceans and allow ships to take much shorter routes to reach certain destinations. Please note that some features extend beyond the grid reference given.

Andrew Brodie: Geography Today 10–11 © A & C Black 2008

Maps — Worksheet 4
Map of the world

Name _____ Date _____

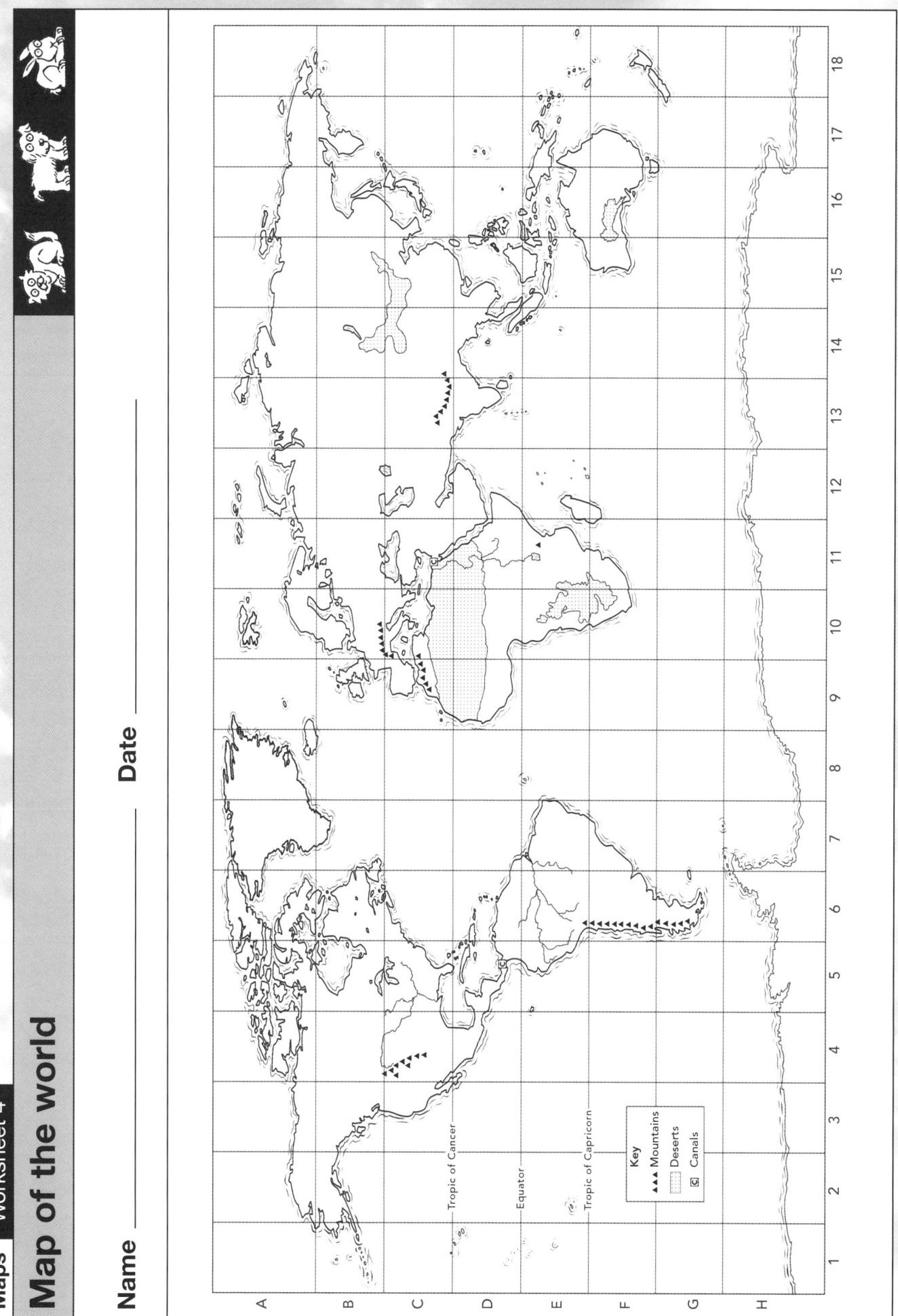

Teachers' notes This worksheet needs to be used in conjunction with Worksheet 3 which gives the grid references to find mountains, rivers and deserts.

Maps Worksheet 5

Can I use map references on a map of Europe?

Name _____ Date _____

Look at the map on Worksheet 6. All of the following cities are marked on the map. Use the grid references shown alongside each city's name to find its correct position on the map. Write the name of each city in the correct place and write the name of the country it is in.

These cities are the capital cities of the three largest countries in the European Union:

Madrid 2B
Paris 4C
Stockholm 5E

These cities are the capital cities of the three countries with the greatest populations in the European Union:

Berlin 5D
Paris 4C
Rome 5B

The biggest country in Europe is also partly in Asia. It is not a member of the European Union. Its capital city is in the block with grid reference 8E. What is the city and what is the country?

City: _____ Country: _____

In the correct places on the map write the names of the following capital cities and the countries that they are in.

Helsinki, Finland 6E
Prague, Czech Republic 5C
Kiev, Ukraine 7D
Athens, Greece 7A

Warsaw, Poland 6D
Oslo, Norway 5E
Reykjavik, Iceland 2G

Write the Mediterranean Sea and the North Sea in the correct places on the map.

The highest mountains in Europe are in a range called the Alps – write the Alps in the correct place.

The River Rhine is an important river in Europe – write the Rhine in the correct place.

Teachers' notes This worksheet needs to be used in conjunction with Worksheet 6, which shows a map of Europe and a grid referencing system. Pupils use the grid references to find cities and countries while learning some of the key geographical facts from the National Curriculum Programmes of Study. This activity is designed for pupils of all abilities but some pupils may need extra support.

Maps | **Worksheet 6**

Map of Europe

Name _____ Date _____

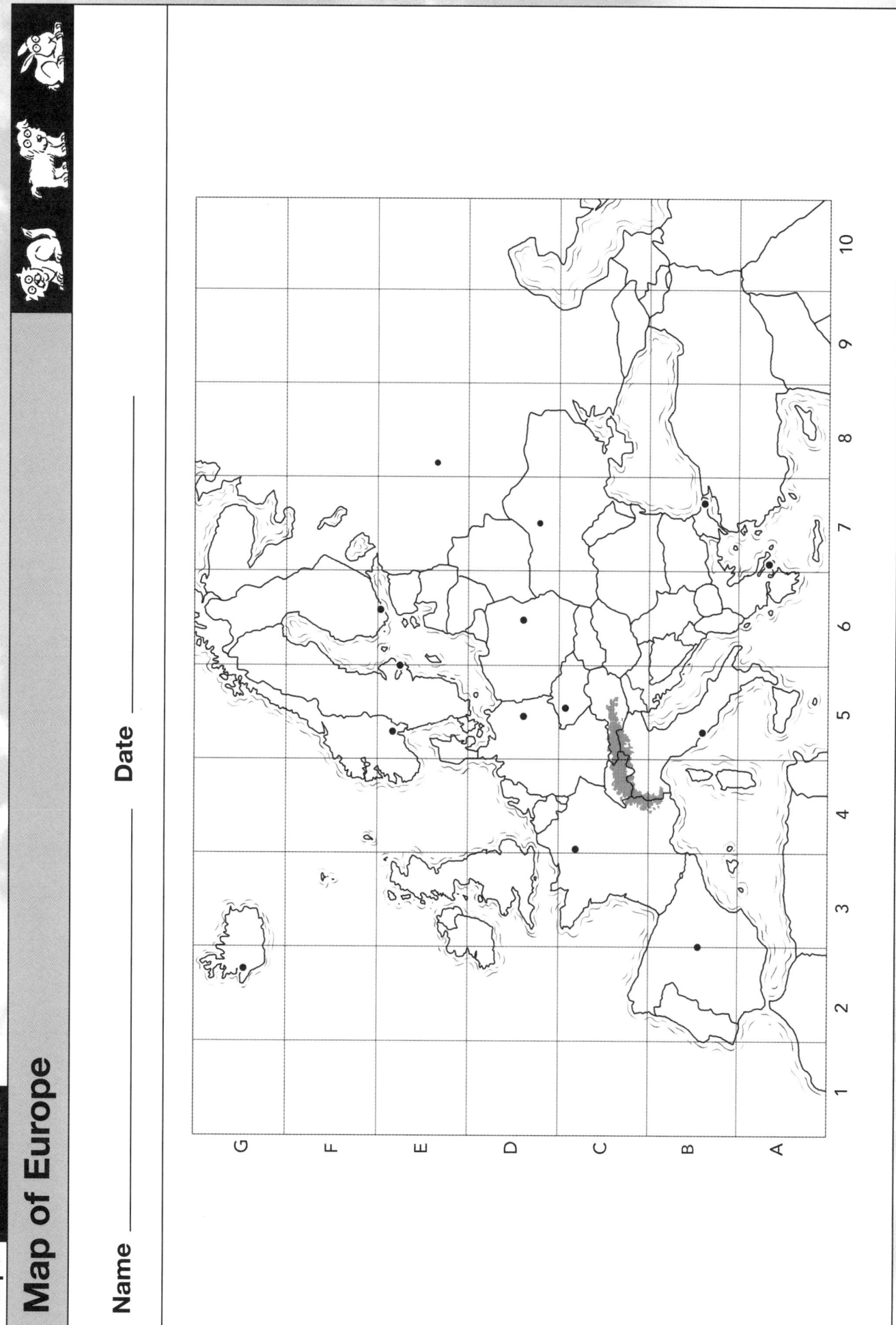

Teachers' notes This worksheet needs to be used in conjunction with Worksheet 5 which gives the grid references to find mountains, rivers and deserts.

Andrew Brodie: Geography Today 10–11 © A & C Black 2008

Maps — Worksheet 7

Can I use map references on a map of the British Isles?

Name _____ Date _____

Look at the map on Worksheet 8. All of the following cities are marked on the map. Use the grid references shown alongside each city's name to find its correct position on the map. Write the name of each city in the correct place and write the name of the country it is in.

These cities are the capital cities of the United Kingdom and the Republic of Ireland:

Belfast 4E   Cardiff 5B   Dublin 3D   Edinburgh 5G   London 7B

Which of these cities is the capital city of a foreign country?

_____

These cities are all in the United Kingdom:

Bristol 6B   Swansea 5B   Liverpool 5D   Birmingham 6C
Manchester 6D   Sheffield 6D   Newcastle Upon Tyne 6F   Norwich 8C
Southampton 6B   Glasgow 5G   Aberdeen 6H   Dundee 6G

Write the Irish Sea, the North Sea and the English Channel in the correct places on the map.

Write the Cambrian Mountains, the Grampian Mountains, the Lake District and the Pennines in the correct places on the map.

Write the River Severn, the River Thames and the River Trent in the correct places on the map.

Teachers' notes This worksheet needs to be used in conjunction with Worksheet 8, which shows a map of the British Isles and a grid referencing system. Pupils use the grid references to find cities and countries while learning some of the key geographical facts from the National Curriculum Programmes of Study. This activity is designed for pupils of all abilities but some pupils may need extra support.

Andrew Brodie: Geography Today 10–11 © A & C Black 2008

Maps Worksheet 8

Map of the British Isles

Name _____ Date _____

Teachers' notes This worksheet needs to be used in conjunction with Worksheet 7 which gives the grid references to find mountains, rivers and deserts.

Maps — Vocabulary sheet 1

equator	tropic	tropical
Cancer	Capricorn	Arctic
Antarctica	Australia	Oceania
Africa	Europe	Asia
north	south	America
continent	cities	countries
grid reference	mountain	desert

Maps	Vocabulary sheet 2	
Brazil	Indonesia	Russia
Canada	Japan	Nigeria
United States	Andes	Atlas
Himalayas	Kilimanjaro	Rocky
Sahara	Kalahari	Gobi
Victoria	Amazon	Mississippi
Nile	Panama	Suez

Maps — Vocabulary sheet 3

France	**Spain**	**Sweden**
Germany	**Italy**	**Stockholm**
Paris	**Madrid**	**Berlin**
Rome	**Poland**	**Mediterranean**
Alps	**Rhine**	**Severn**
Thames	**Trent**	**Cambrian**
Grampian	**Lake District**	**Pennines**

USING ORDNANCE SURVEY MAPS

Contents

This unit focuses on gaining an understanding of how to use local maps, such as Ordnance Survey maps and recognise the Ordnance survey symbols. The CD-ROM presentation introduces map symbols and the worksheets use map symbols and grid references in relation to a map of a small seaside area.

This unit features:
- CD-ROM: USING ORDNANCE SURVEY MAPS 1–16
- Worksheets 1–3

Useful resources

- local area maps
- Ordnance Survey maps

Learning objectives

- asking geographical questions
- using appropriate geographical vocabulary
- using secondary sources of information
- identifying and describing what places are like
- locating and describing where places are
- recognising how places fit within a wider geographical context
- recognising physical and human features in the environment
- using maps and plans at a range of scales.

The worksheets

Worksheet 1: Can I use map symbols?
Worksheet 2: Can I use map symbols to help me find places?
Worksheet 3: Can I use four figure grid references?

CD-ROM

This CD-ROM presentation features the type of symbols that could be found on an Ordnance Survey map. Show the children a copy of a local OS map for your area, pointing out your own town or village before showing them the CD-ROM slides. Explain that the map uses symbols to represent certain features, for example a picnic area – these symbols are shown in a 'key' or 'legend' attached to the map. For each symbol ask the children if they can work out what it means; when rolled over name will appear.

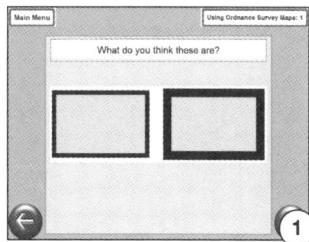

Most buildings are shown from a bird's eye view.

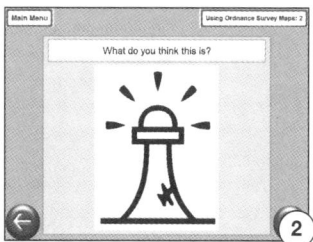

Are there any lighthouses in our area?

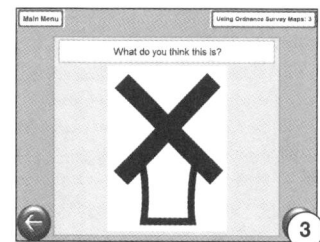

Is there an old windmill in our area? What were windmills used for?

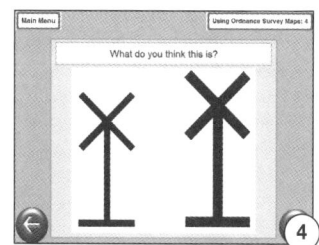

Are there any wind turbines in our area? In what way are they like windmills? In what way are they different to windmills?

The CD-ROM continued

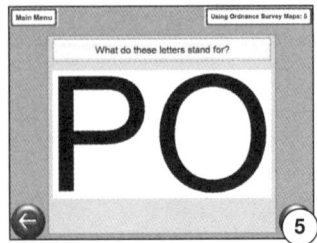

What do these letters stand for? Why would they be shown on a map?

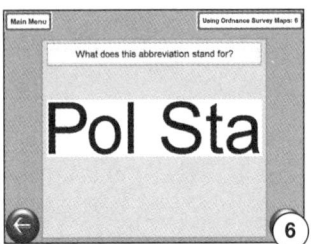

What do these abbreviations stand for? Why would they be shown on a map?

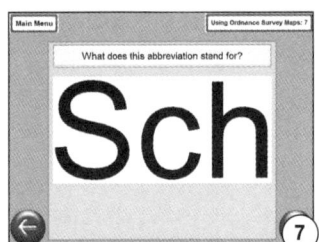

What does this abbreviation stand for?

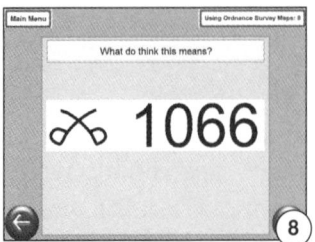

What famous battle took place in 1066? That battle took place in Hastings in Sussex but there are other battle sites in lots of parts of the country. At each site there will be the crossed sword symbol together with a date in brackets. Has there been a battle in our area? If so when did it take place?

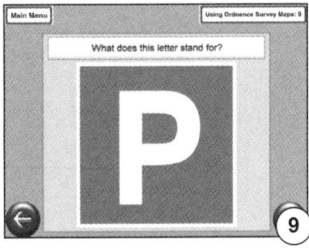

What does this letter stand for?

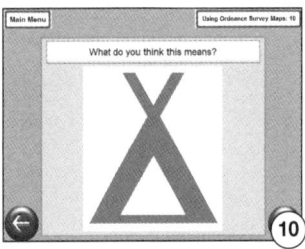

Are there any camp sites in our area? Where would the nearest camp site be? Do any of you go camping? Where do you go?

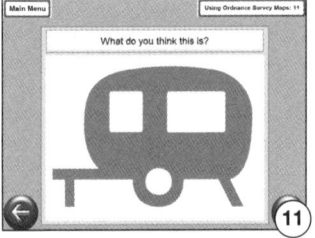

Where would the nearest caravan site be to this school? Are there many caravan sites in our area? Why?

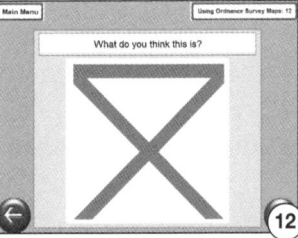

Can you think of any picnic sites that you have seen? Where have you seen one? Why is it helpful to show picnic sites on a map?

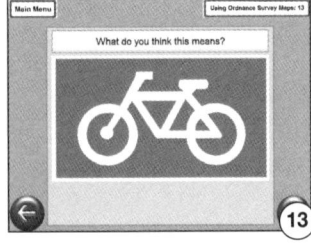

Cycle trails are becoming very popular. Why do you think this is? Can you think of a cycle trail in our area?

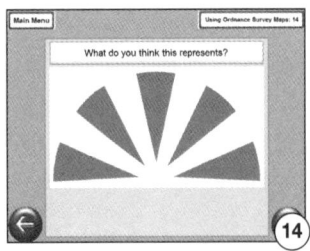

What is a viewpoint? Where might you find one? Can you think of one near here?

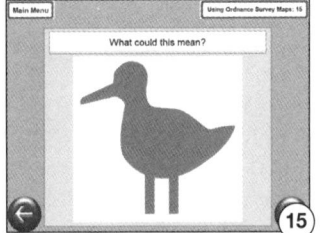

The symbol shows a bird but most nature reserves are not just for birds. What is a nature reserve? Do you know where there is one?

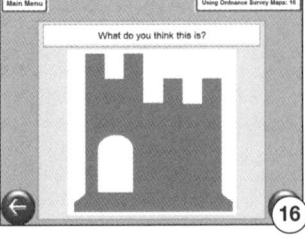

Are there any castles or forts in our area? Have you ever visited a castle? Have you ever visited a fort? What's the difference between a castle and a fort?

Teachers' notes There are, of course, other symbols on maps and you may wish to show your pupils the complete key of an Ordnance Survey map, perhaps paying particular attention to key features for your area. If you have other maps available you could point out the different symbols used. Pupils can now complete the worksheets.

Ordnance Survey maps — Worksheet 1

Can I use map symbols?

Name _____ Date _____

Write the correct description for each map symbol shown.
The words you need are in the word bank.

buildings	lighthouse	windmill	wind turbine	Post Office	Police Station
school	battle	parking	camp site	caravan site	picnic site
cycle trail	viewpoint	nature reserve	castle/fort		

Teachers' notes This task follows the CD-ROM presentation of the ordnance survey symbols. It would be helpful for pupils to examine a real Ordnance Survey map to try to find places where the symbols appear. An extension activity could be for the pupils to draw a sketch map of a real or imaginary area, using some of the symbols that they have learnt.

Andrew Brodie: Geography Today 10–11 © A & C Black 2008

Ordnance Survey maps — Worksheet 2

Can I use map symbols to help me find places?

Name _____ Date _____

Use the map below to help you to answer the questions.

[Map showing grid references 32-38 horizontally and 16-20 vertically, with features including Ham Castle, Ham Farm, Bay Farm, Combe Farm, Hamcombe, North Bay, South Bay, Ham Head, Stacy's Stacks, Shark Island. Scale: 0–5km]

Key:
- buildings
- parking (P)
- lighthouse
- camp site
- windmill
- caravan site
- wind turbine
- picnic site
- Post Office (PO)
- cycle trail
- Police Station (Pol Sta)
- viewpoint
- school (Sch)
- nature reserve
- 1066 battle
- castle/fort
- road
- footpath

In what village is the school situated? _____

At what farm could you have a caravan holiday? _____

In what year did a battle take place? _____

At what farm could you stay in a tent? _____

What farm is south of Ham Farm? _____

Where could you get a view across the sea? _____

What would you find to the southwest of the school? _____

What would you see to the southeast of the picnic site? _____

Colour the sea blue. Colour the roads red. Colour the beaches yellow. Colour the land green.

Teachers' notes This task involves the use of some of the symbols introduced in the CD-ROM presentation. It would be helpful for pupils to examine a real Ordnance Survey map to try to find places where the symbols appear. An extension activity would be for the pupils to draw a sketch map of a real or imaginary area, using some of the symbols that they have learnt.

Ordnance Survey maps Worksheet 3

Can I use four figure grid references?

Name _____ **Date** _____

We can use grid references to explain where places are on the map.
Four-figure grid references are used to identify the lower left-hand corner of a square.
For example, we say that the school is in square 34 17.

➡ 34 Look across the page to find the first number.

⬆ 17 Look up the page to find the second number.

Give the four-figure grid references for the following places:

Shark Island ☐☐☐☐   Nature reserve ☐☐☐☐   Wind turbines ☐☐☐☐
Ham Castle ☐☐☐☐   North Bay Beach ☐☐☐☐   Stacy's Stacks ☐☐☐☐

Draw symbols for the following extra features on the map:

A picnic site in square 36 19.
Four wind turbines in square 32 20.

A caravan site in square 33 20.
A site of a battle dated 1644 in square 32 16.

Teachers' notes This task involves the use of some of the symbols introduced in the CD-ROM presentation but also extends pupils' skills by considering four-figure grid references. It would be helpful for pupils to examine a real Ordnance Survey map to try to find places where the symbols appear. An extension activity would be for the pupils to draw a sketch map of a real or imaginary area, using some of the symbols that they have learnt.

LOCAL MAPS

Contents

This unit focuses on gaining an understanding of how to use local maps, such as Ordnance Survey maps. The CD-ROM presentation provides revision of points of the compass and further work on grid references, introducing six figure grid references, as well as work on scale. The worksheets use grid references, points of a compass and scale in relation to a map of a small seaside area.

This unit features:
- CD-ROM: LOCAL MAPS 1–16
- Worksheets 1–3

Useful resources

- local area maps
- Ordnance Survey maps
- rulers

Learning objectives

- asking geographical questions
- using appropriate geographical vocabulary
- using maps and plans at a range of scales
- using secondary sources of information
- drawing maps and plans at a range of scales
- identifying and describing what places are like
- locating and describing where places are
- recognising how places fit within a wider geographical context
- recognising physical and human features in the environment

The worksheets

Worksheet 1: Can I use compass directions?
Worksheet 2: Can I use the scale on the map?
Worksheet 3: Can I use six figure grid references?

CD-ROM

This CD-ROM presentation provides revision of points of the compass and further work on grid references, introducing six figure grid references, as well as work on scale.

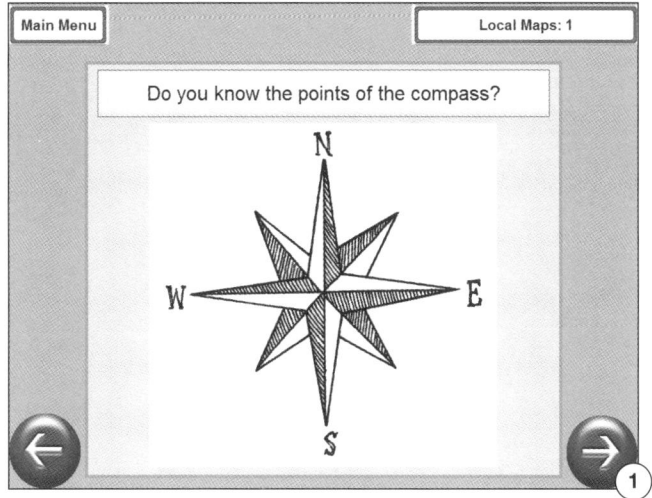

Discuss the points of the compass with the pupils – can they all remember the positions of the four key directions? They may like to use 'Naughty Elephants Squirt Water' but may prefer to invent their own mnemonic. Once these are established can they identify the 'between' directions: North-West, North-East, South-West, South-East? Can they use compass directions to describe what part of the country they live in? Discuss the use of the word 'due' meaning 'directly' in relation to compass directions. Worksheet 1 provides practice in using compass directions to show relative positions.

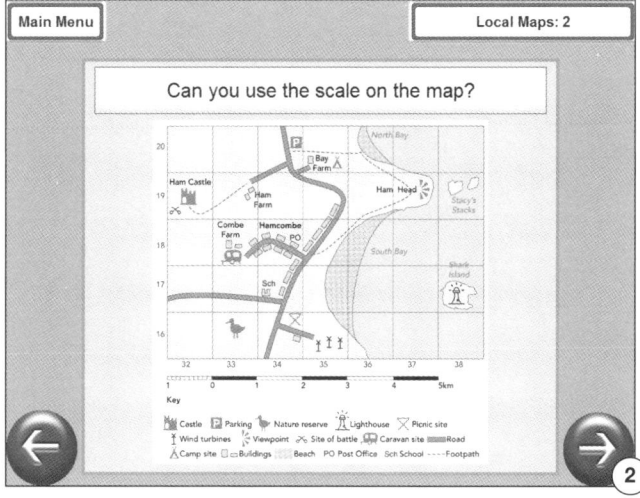

Discuss the scale bar with the pupils. Show them how the bar is like a number line from 0 to 5 but also shows the negative 1 position to show smaller calibrations. Explain that each large step represents one kilometre so the distance from the 0 to the 5 is a total of 5 kilometres – ask the pupils what each of the smaller calibrations represents and they should be able to work out that it is 100 metres. Point out that the grid on the map is arranged to match the scale bar so every square is 1 kilometre by 1 kilometre. This can be useful for finding distances between places: roughly how far is it from the school to the post office 'as the crow flies'? Note that if you wanted to walk from the school to the post office it would be further. Worksheet 2 gives practice in finding distances on the map.

Remind the pupils how to use four figure grid references. Mention some of the places shown on the map and ask them to give the four figure references for these: the school, for example, is in grid square 3417. Notice that the 'eastings' are given before the 'northings' – ie 34 East then 17 North. A mnemonic, shared with coordinates in maths, is to say 'along the corridor and up the stairs'.

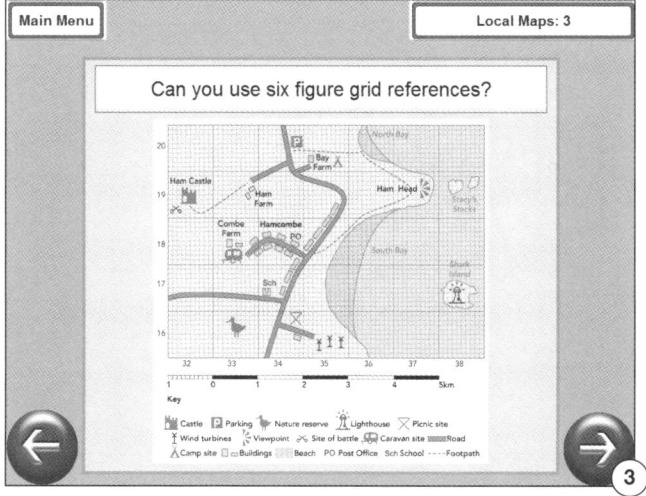

This activity is designed to extend more able pupils. Tell the pupils that now you are going to look at six figure grid references. Click the mouse to show the overlay grid – explain that this would not appear on a map but it shows what you have to do. Look at the square the school is in, which is given by the four figure grid reference 3417. A more accurate position of the school would be 342 174 – line 34 then 2 tenths of the next grid square in the eastings direction and line 17 then 4 tenths of the next square in the northings direction.

Local Maps Worksheet 1

Can I use compass directions?

Name _____ Date _____

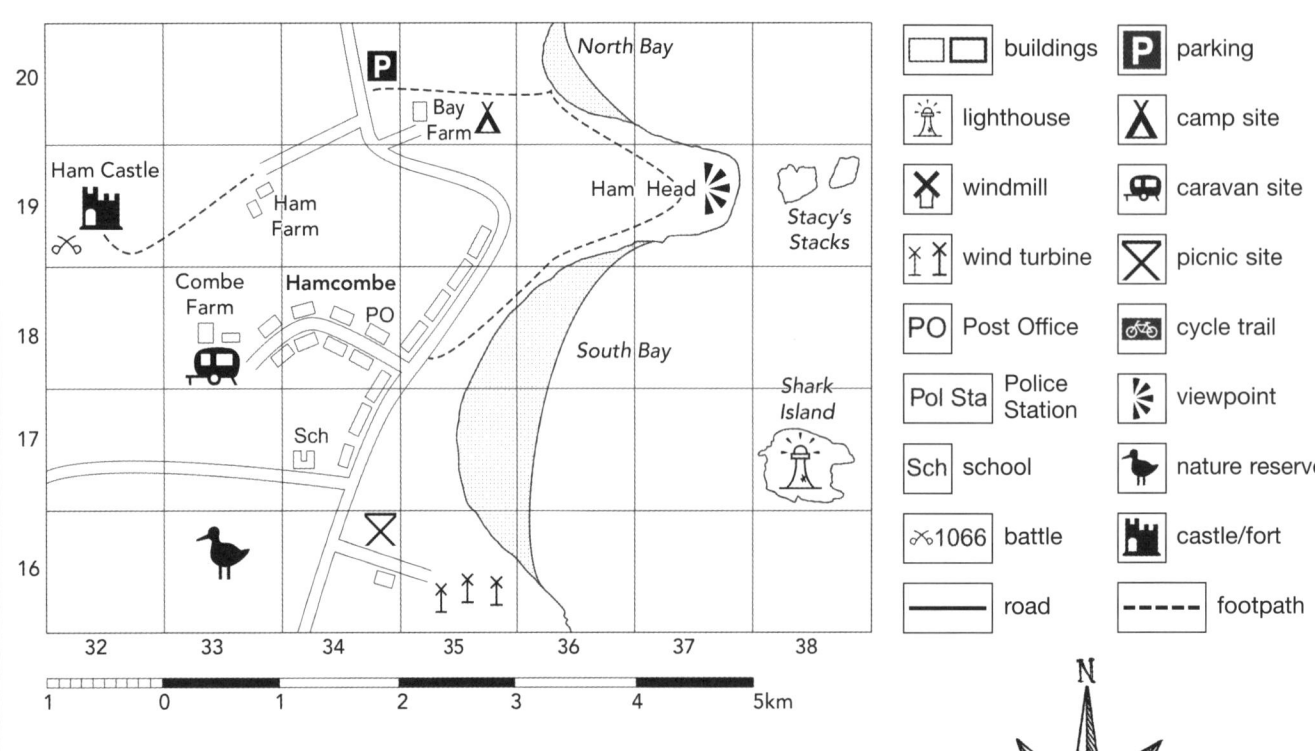

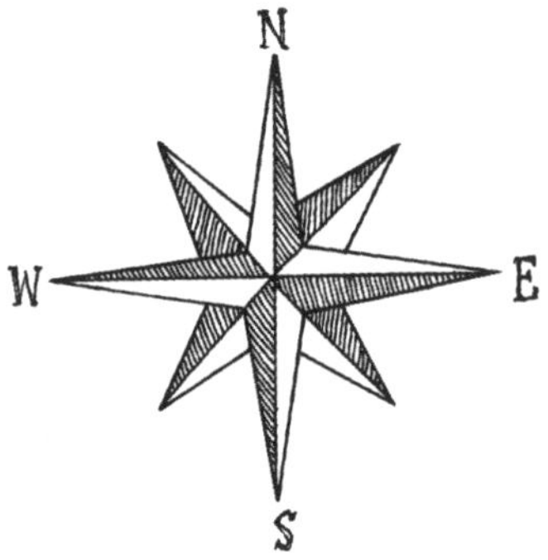

What physical feature is east of Ham Head? _____

What is south-east of Ham Head? _____

What might I find at the place which is south-west of the school? _____

If I was at Ham Castle, in what direction would I face to see Combe Farm? _____

Which bay is due east of Hamcombe? _____

In what direction is North Bay from Hamcombe? _____

Teachers' notes This worksheet can be used after the pupils have seen the CD-ROM presentation.

Local Maps | **Worksheet 2**

Can I use the scale on the map?

Name _____ Date _____

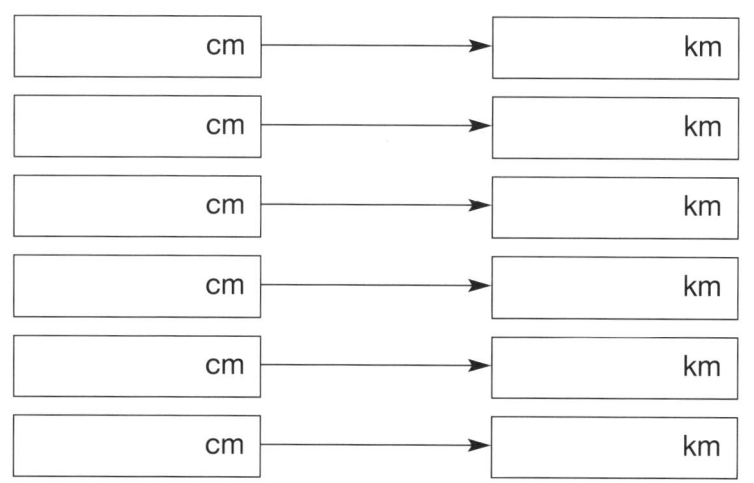

The map is drawn to the scale of 2 cm : 1 km.
This means that 2 cm on the map represents 1 km. 1 cm would show $\frac{1}{2}$ km or 500 metres.

Use your ruler to measure the distances below 'as the crow flies'. Give your answer to the nearest centimetre then work out the actual distances that your measurements represent.

From Combe Farm to the post office	cm	km
From the wind turbines to Ham Head	cm	km
From Shark Island to Stacy's Stacks	cm	km
From Bay Farm to Combe Farm	cm	km
From the school to the castle	cm	km
From the caravan site to the camp site	cm	km

Teachers' notes This worksheet can be used by higher ability pupils after they have seen the CD-ROM presentation.

Andrew Brodie: Geography Today 10–11 © A & C Black 2008

Local Maps — Worksheet 3

Can I use six figure grid references?

Name _____ Date _____

The school is in grid square 34 17. Its six figure grid reference is 342 174. This is because it is approximately $\frac{2}{10}$ of the way between line 34 and line 35 and $\frac{4}{10}$ of the way between line 17 and line 18.

Give the six figure grid references of each of the places below.

Ham Castle _____

The lighthouse on Shark Island _____

The picnic site _____

The farmhouse at Bay Farm _____

The post office _____

The caravan site _____

Teachers' notes This worksheet can be used by higher ability pupils after they have seen the CD-ROM presentation.

Andrew Brodie: Geography Today 10–11 © A & C Black 2008

THE POWER OF THE WIND

Contents

This unit provides an opportunity for the pupils to debate a potentially contentious issue - the construction of a wind farm in the local area. The Primary Framework for literacy suggests that Year 6 pupils should:

- use a range of oral techniques to present persuasive arguments
- participate in whole class debate using the conventions and language of debate, including standard English
- use the techniques of dialogic talk to explore ideas, topics or issues
- consider examples of conflict and resolution, exploring the language used
- understand and use a variety of ways to criticise constructively and respond to criticism

This unit features:
- CD-ROM: POWER OF THE WIND 1–4
- Worksheets 1–3
- Vocabulary sheet 1

Useful resources

- map of the local area

Learning objectives

- asking geographical questions
- using appropriate geographical vocabulary
- collecting and recording evidence
- analysing evidence and drawing conclusions
- identifying and explaining different views that people, including themselves, hold about topical geographical issues
- communicating in ways appropriate to the task and audience
- using secondary sources of information
- using decision-making skills
- identifying how and why places change and how they may change in the future
- recognising physical and human features in the environment
- recognising how people can improve the environment or damage it, and how decisions about places and environments affect the future quality of people's lives
- studying an environmental issue

The worksheets

Worksheet 1: How is wind power used?
Worksheet 2: How is wind power used?
Worksheet 3: How do I feel about the wind farm?

The vocabulary sheet

The vocabulary sheet can be photocopied then made into flashcards, which can be used for both geography and literacy. It would be helpful to read through the vocabulary with the pupils ensuring that they understand what each word means and why it is relevant to this subject.

CD-ROM

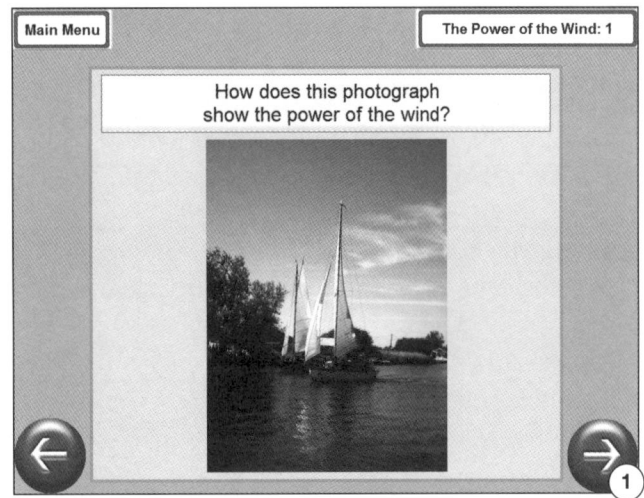

Encourage the pupils to answer the question. Hopefully they can see that these boats are travelling purely through harnessing wind power. *For thousands of years most sea travel was possible through the use of wind power and, unlike the boats in the picture, the sailing ships had no motorised backup to deal with calm days. Very few ships are now powered by the wind but are instead using fossil fuels to power their engines.*

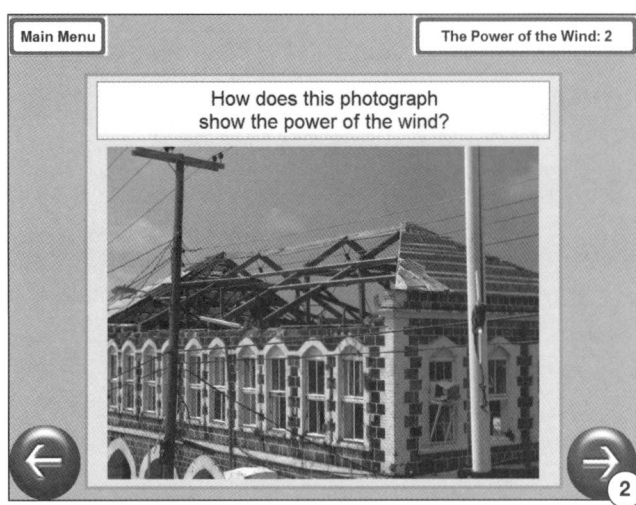

Here the power of the wind was more destructive. This roof on a building on the island of Grenada was damaged by a hurricane. Ask the children if they know where Grenada is and some may be able to identify it as an island in the Caribbean, an area prone to hurricanes – you may like to take the opportunity to ask pupils to locate the Caribbean on a world map. You may also wish to discuss any recent hurricanes that have been reported on the news.

Hopefully pupils will recognise this as a wind farm – ask the children why this is perhaps a strange use of the word 'farm'. Discuss the photograph, encouraging them to notice that the wind turbines are not on land. This photograph was taken in Norfolk and you may like to take the opportunity to ask pupils to find Norfolk on a map of the United Kingdom.

Ask the pupils to compare this photograph to the previous one – what differences do they notice? The most significant difference, of course, is that the wind turbines here are on land. Ask the children to look closely at the picture – can they see other things that give them an idea of the size of the turbines?

Ask the pupils what the purpose of the wind turbines is – why are they there? They will probably be aware that the turbines produce electricity. Discuss other methods of producing electricity – burning fuels such as coal, gas or oil; nuclear reactors; water powered turbines. Which of these cause least harm to the environment?

Encourage the children to begin to develop ideas for debate: what are the good things about wind turbines? What are the negative aspects? Some people feel strongly that wind turbines should be widely used for electricity generation as they are environmentally friendly – others feel that they are a 'blot on the landscape', that they are too noisy and that they are dangerous to birds.

The Power of the Wind Worksheet 2

How is wind power used?

Name _____ Date _____

How has wind power been used by people for thousands of years?
_____
_____

In what way can the power of the wind be dangerous?
_____
_____

What do wind turbines and wind farms produce for us?
_____
_____

Why might people be pleased to have a wind farm nearby?
_____
_____

Why might people not be pleased to have a wind farm nearby?
_____
_____

Teachers' notes This worksheet can be completed after the pupils have seen and discussed the CD-ROM presentation.

The Power of the Wind — Worksheet 2
How is wind power used?

Name _____   Date _____

Work with a partner so that you can discuss ideas.

Imagine that a new wind farm is to be built very near to your school. It will have four wind turbines and each one will be approximately 100 metres tall. Now consider the people who live and work in your area. Which people will be pleased about the new wind farm and why will they be pleased? Which people will not be pleased and why?

Start with listing the people who live and work in your area. Here are some ideas: families, school children, farmers, teachers, factory workers, factory owners, doctors and nurses, shopkeepers, office workers, builders, councillors.

_____   _____   _____
_____   _____   _____
_____   _____   _____
_____   _____   _____
_____   _____   _____
_____   _____   _____

Now try to work out whether you think any of these groups of people will be pleased about the wind farm or not pleased. Sort the people into two sets.

Can you sum up why some people might be pleased about the new wind farm and why some people might not be pleased? You may need to use the back of the sheet.

pleased	not pleased

Teachers' notes Pupils need to work with a partner to gain the maximum value out of this speaking and listening activity. Once the partners have agreed their ideas they could share them with the rest of the class.

Andrew Brodie: Geography Today 10–11 © A & C Black 2008

The Power of the Wind | Worksheet 3

How do I feel about the wind farm?

Name _____ **Date** _____

Imagine that a new wind farm is to be built very near to your school. It will have four wind turbines and each one will be approximately 100 metres tall. You are going to present a speech to a meeting of local people to try to persuade them either that the wind farm is a good idea or that it is a bad idea. Decide now which side of the argument you are going to support and consider some reasons why you have chosen this. When you are ready, draft out your speech below.

_____
_____
_____
_____
_____
_____
_____
_____
_____
_____
_____
_____
_____
_____
_____

Teachers' notes Higher ability pupils should attempt this exercise after they have seen the presentation and have completed worksheet 2. Once they have created their speeches you may like to hold a 'public meeting' in the class, at which the pupils present both sides of the argument. The other pupils could then vote for or against the wind farm.

The Power of the Wind — Vocabulary sheet 1

turbine	energy	generator
electricity	onshore	offshore
sailing	hurricane	Grenada
Norfolk	local	debate
argument	decisions	business
factory	council	councillor
nuclear	fossil fuel	environment

RIVERS

Contents

By looking at rivers in this country and abroad we are able to encourage pupils to look more closely at a local river. Where is its source? Where does it flow to? What are different sections of the river like? Does it flood? Does it carry traffic? Do any important bridges cross it? Pupils can use local maps to examine the route of the river. If possible, you might wish to arrange a visit to your local river (after appropriate risk assessments). It is essential to remind pupils of the dangers of rivers and other stretches of water.

Pupils are introduced to some of the special terminology we might use in relation to rivers and an extension activity invites pupils to research information about one of the world's most famous rivers. This unit also revises the water cycle, first covered in our unit on water in Geography Today for ages 9–10, and pupils also consider why people may have chosen to build settlements close to rivers.

This unit features:
- CD-ROM: RIVERS 1–20
- Worksheets 1–8
- Vocabulary sheet

Useful resources

- map of the local area
- world map and globe

Learning objectives

- asking geographical questions
- using appropriate geographical vocabulary
- collecting and recording evidence
- analysing evidence and drawing conclusions
- communicating in ways appropriate to the task and audience
- using secondary sources of information
- using ICT to help in geographical investigations
- drawing plans and maps at a range of scales
- using decision-making skills
- identifying and describing what places are like
- locating places and environments
- identifying how and why places change and how they may change in the future
- recognising physical and human features in the environment
- recognising how people can improve the environment or damage it, and how decisions about places and environments affect the future quality of people's lives
- identifying the physical features of rivers
- studying an environmental issue

The worksheets

Worksheet 1: What special words may be used about rivers?
Worksheet 2: What special words about rivers do I know?
Worksheet 3: What special words about rivers do I know?
Worksheet 4: What do I know about my local river?
Worksheet 5: Can I describe the water cycle?
Worksheet 6: Why did early settlers choose to live by rivers?
Worksheet 7: Why did early settlers choose to live by rivers?
Worksheet 8: What can I discover about a famous river?

Vocabulary sheet

The sheet can also be photocopied then made into flashcards, which can be used for both geography and literacy. It would be helpful to read through the vocabulary with the pupils ensuring that they understand what each word means and why it is relevant to this subject.

CD-ROM

This CD-ROM presentation features photographs of different rivers in the United Kingdom to illustrate the stages that one river may go through from its source to its mouth. Discuss with the children that not every river has every feature but by looking at several rivers we can see many of the main features that occur.

Remind the pupils that water evaporates from the surface of the sea; the water vapour rises and forms clouds, which are blown over the land by the wind. As they reach land the clouds rise up and the water droplets bunch together until they are heavy enough to fall as rain. This photograph shows clouds crossing the Brecon Beacons in South Wales and clearly rain is about to fall. Ask the children what would happen to the rain water once it has fallen on the hills. Encourage them to realise that some will soak into the ground and some will run off into streams. The water that has soaked in will emerge in springs from the ground lower down the slope.

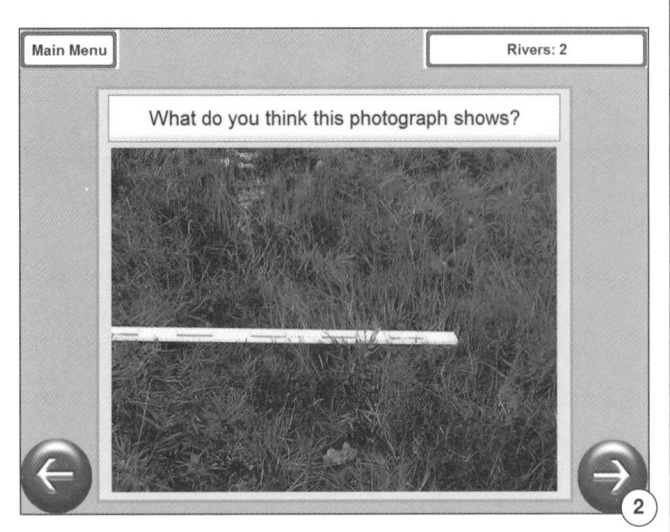

This photograph was taken at the source of a river in Somerset, England. High up in the hills water has soaked into the ground then come out of the ground through springs. The water has gathered in puddles and small amounts of water drain from one into another one slightly lower down the slope. The metre rule gives some idea of scale. The water gathers momentum and begins to flow and over a distance of about 100 metres a small stream begins.

Encourage the pupils to answer the question in relation to what has happened to the water: some of the smaller streams have met together and formed a larger stream. A smaller stream or river that joins a larger stream or river is called a tributary. Does your local river have a tributary nearby? Is your local river a tributary of another river? Look at a local map to find out.

Discuss what the picture shows. The stream is running quickly down a valley between hills; other tributaries join it and add more water so that the stream becomes wider and deeper. Sometimes the water will be strong enough to move rocks and stones. This stream is in Wales.

The CD-ROM continued

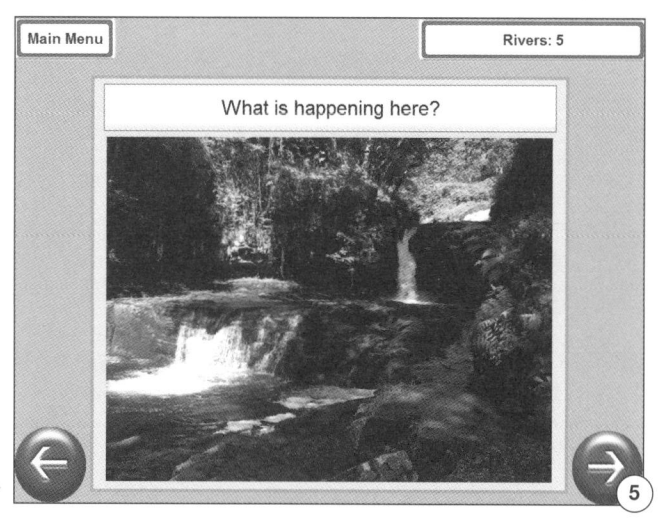

Rivers: 5 — What is happening here?

This Welsh stream is now wider and is following the slope of the valley. Sometimes the valley floor drops sharply and waterfalls are formed. Can the pupils think of any waterfalls near the school or that they have visited on holiday? If they have visited waterfalls do they remember where they were? Can they find the places on a map? Can they look them up on the internet?

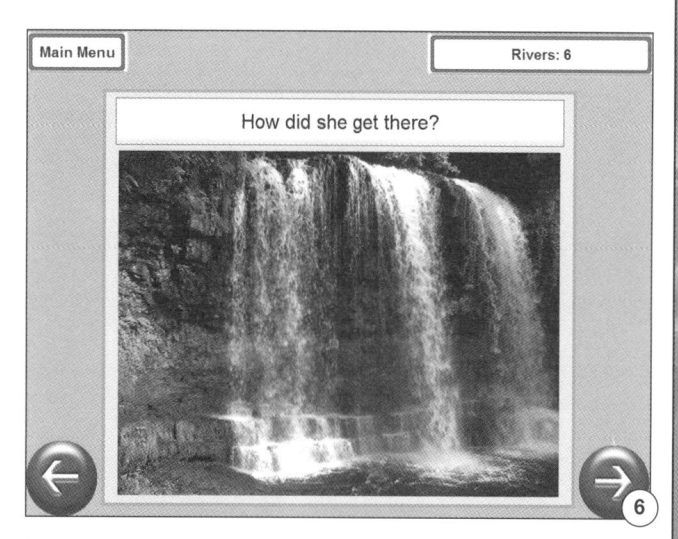

Rivers: 6 — How did she get there?

You may wish to discuss water safety and explain that there is a path behind this waterfall in Wales.

Can the pupils estimate how tall the waterfall is? They could estimate the height of the woman first then decide how many times her height the waterfall is. Encourage the children to notice that the river is much bigger here as other streams have joined the main river – can they remember the special name for streams or rivers that join bigger streams or rivers?

Rivers: 7 — Why is this river moving so slowly?

Encourage the pupils to compare this picture to the last two. This is a stream called the Westford Stream in Somerset. The water is moving slowly because there is not such a steep slope. Notice how the river is not moving in a straight line – this wandering movement is known as meandering and a bend in the river like this is called a meander. As always, encourage the children to observe the photograph very carefully – what can they see? They may spot the litter in the water. Litter and pollution are problems in many rivers and cause danger to wildlife.

Rivers: 8 — What's in the river?

How can the pupils tell that this photograph was taken near to a town or village? Can they describe the litter, ie a plastic bag and some polystyrene? Is there litter in the river or stream near your school? Note that the yellow material is a barrier that has been put into the stream to prevent erosion of the river bank – the children will see the effects of erosion in a later slide. If the pupils observe carefully they will see some plant life growing in the river.

The CD-ROM continued

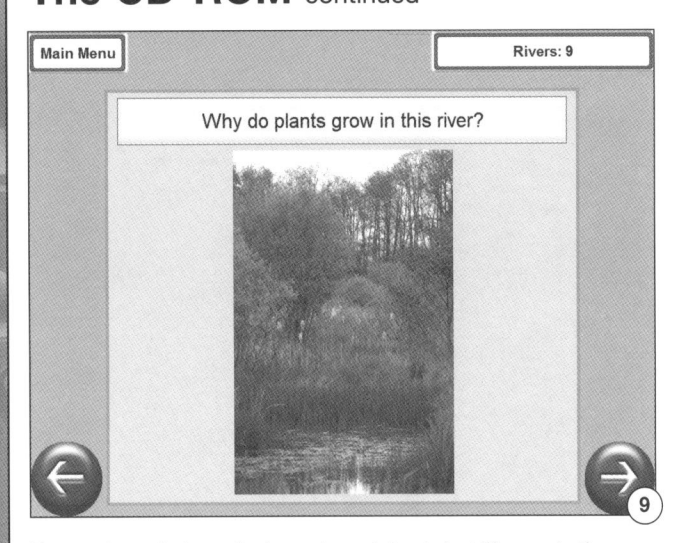

Rivers: 9 — Why do plants grow in this river?

The previous photographs have shown lots of plant life near to the streams and rivers but not much has been growing in them. Can the pupils explain why there are plants growing in this river? They may need some prompting to realise that the water here is so slow moving that reeds and rushes can grow. Is the river near your school fast-moving or slow-moving? Do many plants grow in it?

Rivers: 10 — What is happening here?

This photograph contrasts with the last one and shows a fast moving stretch of a small river. Can the pupils observe that the meandering river is undercutting the bank on the left-hand side of the picture yet dropping soil on the river bed on the right-hand side of the picture? This is because the water on the outside of the bend is moving faster than the water on the inside of the bend. The fast water cuts into the bank, which eventually drops into the stream and gets washed away – this process is called erosion. The slow water drops sediment on to the river bed – this process is called deposition.

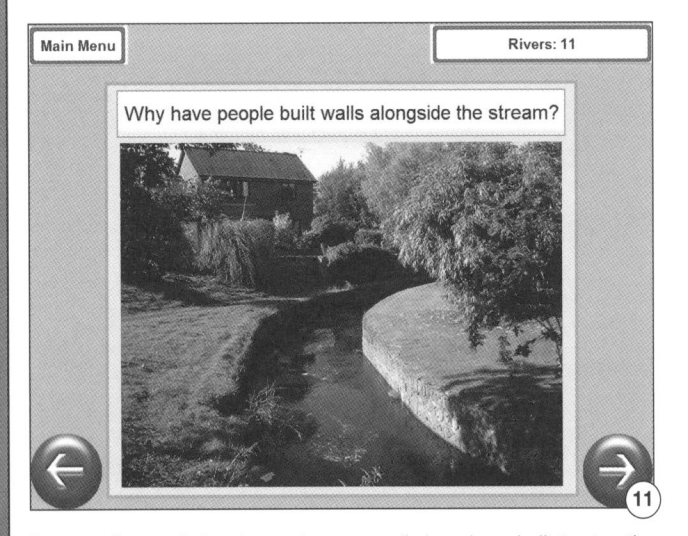

Rivers: 11 — Why have people built walls alongside the stream?

Because the small river is near houses, walls have been built to stop the process of erosion – ask the children why. You may wish to remind the pupils of the yellow barrier that could be seen on one of the previous slides. Again, this was used near houses. Does your local river have any walls or barriers to prevent erosion?

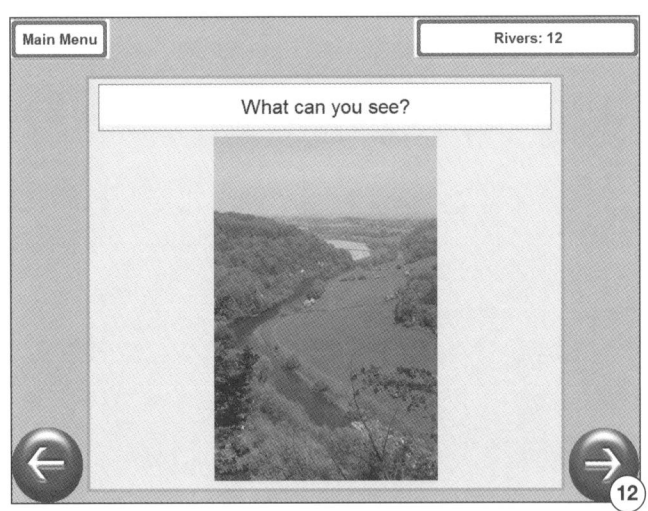

Rivers: 12 — What can you see?

This photograph of the River Wye shows a meander – observant pupils may notice the growth of new grass on the deposition area on the inside of the meander. Ask the pupils to find the location of the River Wye and to look carefully at the river on a map. If your school is licensed to do so the pupils could also look at the River Wye on Google Earth or a similar site.

The CD-ROM continued

Rivers: 13 — Who lives in or on the river?

This photograph is a useful reminder to the pupils that the river provides the habitats for a variety of wildlife. What else could live in or on the river? What wildlife depends on your local river?

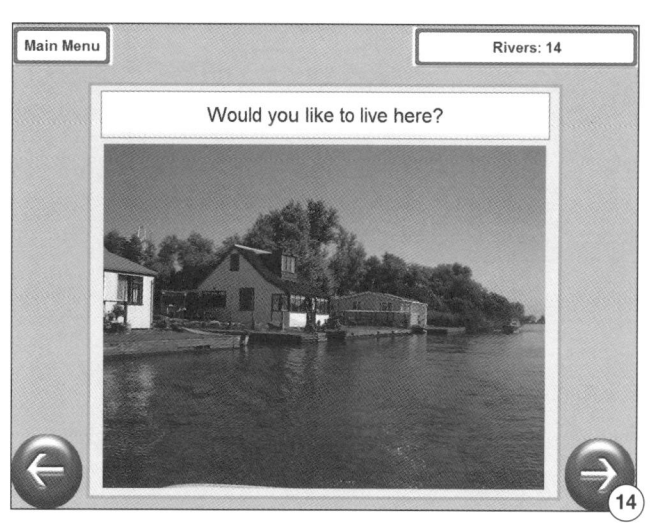

Rivers: 14 — Would you like to live here?

The children may see many attractions to living alongside the river: peace and tranquility, the novelty of travel by water. However, there are potential problems too. These houses by a river in Norfolk could at some time become flooded. Pupils may also suggest other 'problems' caused by the fact that the houses cannot be reached by road – the only access is via a rear footpath or by boat.

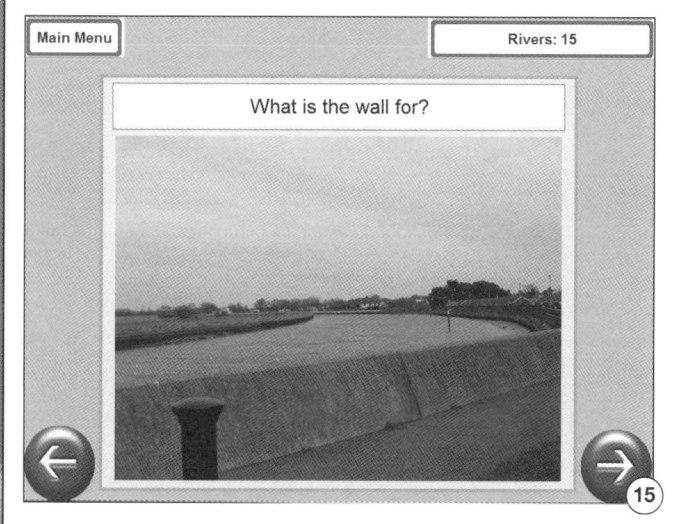

Rivers: 15 — What is the wall for?

Encourage the pupils to look carefully at the picture. Do they notice the houses and bungalows? Can they think of more than one reason the wall could be there? It could be there to prevent erosion of the river bank and it could be there to prevent flooding of the homes nearby. Is there a river near you that could flood? As rivers get closer to the sea a floodplain may develop. Is there a floodplain near your school?

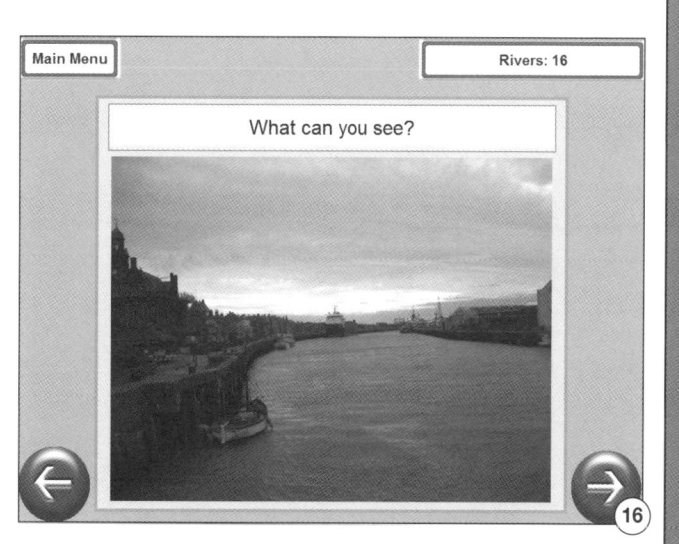

Rivers: 16 — What can you see?

Again, close observation will help the children to notice that this is a wide river; there is at least one cargo boat; there are large protective walls; there is a crane for loading and unloading cargo; there are storage warehouses. Here the pupils can see that the river is near its mouth and is used for trade. (Ensure that pupils are aware that the place where a river enters the sea is called the mouth of the river.) This is the town of Great Yarmouth in Norfolk.

The CD-ROM continued

Rivers: 17 — Where do you think this is?

This is in Great Yarmouth as well. Ask the pupils to describe what they can see. They may be able to identify the overgrown area as a place where the river may flood. They may notice the litter. They may notice the banks and the walls for flood protection. They may notice the poles in the river, some of which have depth markers on them.

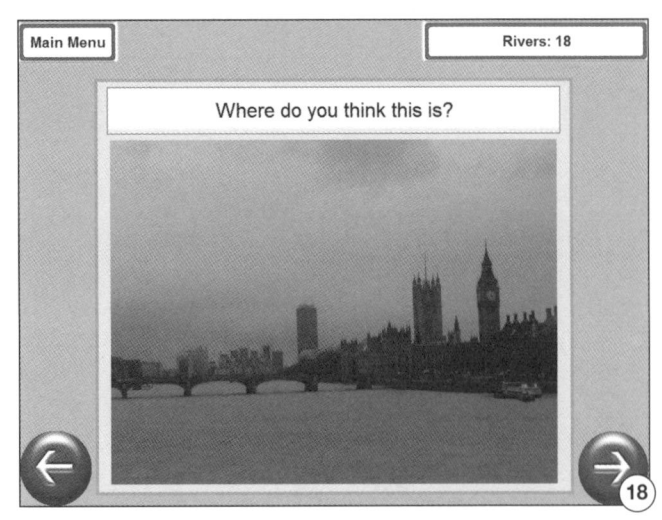

Rivers: 18 — Where do you think this is?

Ask the pupils to identify the river, the bridge and the buildings. They may also be able to explain where the picture was taken from – some reflections that appear on the picture may give them the necessary clue to work out that the photograph was taken from inside a pod on the London Eye.

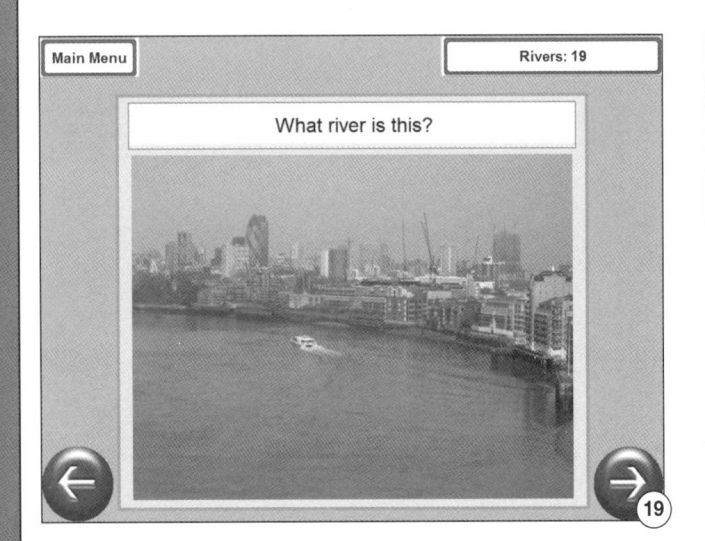

Rivers: 19 — What river is this?

The buildings will probably be the clue that tells the pupils that this is also the River Thames in London. The marks on the sea walls show that the river is tidal – the river, of course, discharges its water into the sea at its mouth but the sea water flows some way up the river with the high tide.

Rivers: 20 — What are the boats doing?

Pupils should look carefully at the picture to observe features such as the London Eye in the distance. They may notice that the boats are all pleasure boats. At one time the River Thames in London would have been a major hub for international trade but this role is now less important.

Rivers Worksheet 1

What special words may be used about rivers?

Name _____ Date _____

Write the correct word, from the river below, underneath each definition.

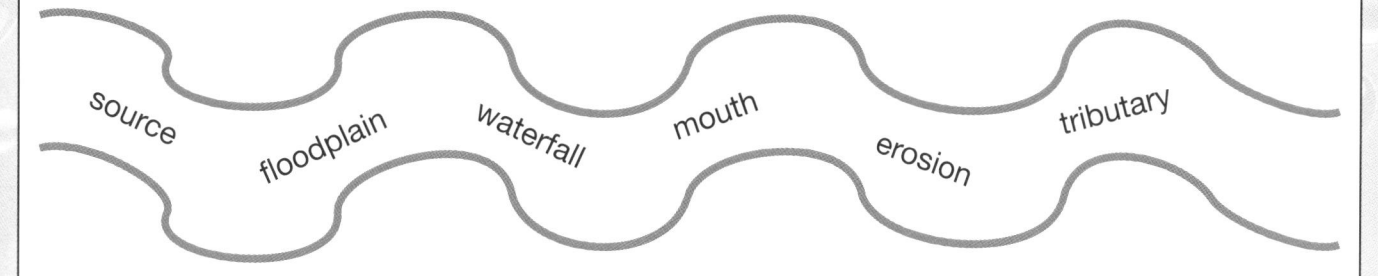

source   floodplain   waterfall   mouth   erosion   tributary

The wearing away of a river bank or river bed by the force of the moving water.

_____

The starting point of a river, often on a mountain or hill.

_____

An area of flat land by the side of a river.

_____

A stream or small river that joins a larger one.

_____

A place where the river falls vertically to a lower level.

_____

The place where a river meets the sea.

_____

Can you think of any other special words about rivers that you may have learnt?

_____
_____

Teachers' notes The children may need to view the presentation more than once and will need to listen carefully to your discussion and explanation so that they hear the key terms that are featured on this worksheet. Some children may benefit from working in a small group with an adult to guide them through the presentation.

Rivers Worksheet 2

What special words about rivers do I know?

Name __Sophia__ Date __11/1/23__

Solve the clues to complete the crossword.
The words you will need are given in the clouds below.

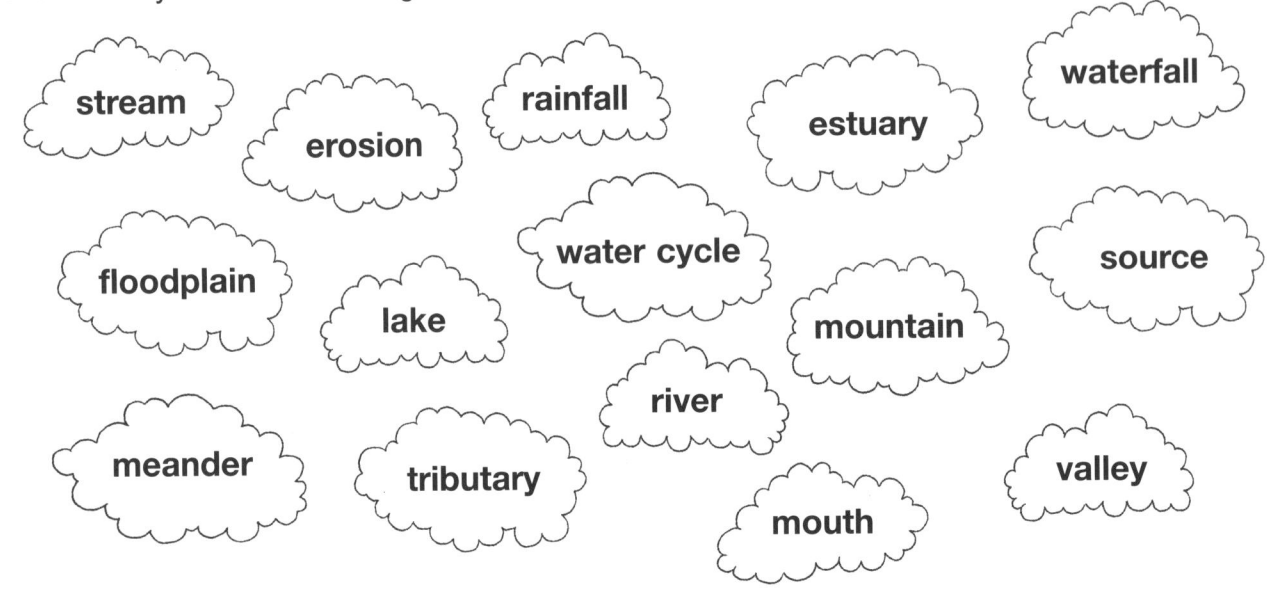

- stream
- erosion
- rainfall
- estuary
- waterfall
- floodplain
- lake
- water cycle
- mountain
- source
- meander
- tributary
- river
- mouth
- valley

Clues Across

2 A stream or small river that joins a larger one.
6 The way water circulates from the seas and rivers, to the clouds and fall to the ground again as rain.
7 The wearing away of rocks and soils.
11 The widening area of water where the river reaches the sea.
12 Larger than a hill, rivers often have their source here.
13 This is formed between two areas of higher land and may have a river running along its floor.
14 A large area of inland water.
15 An area of flat land by the side of a river.

Clues down

1 A place where the river falls vertically to a lower level
3 The course of water that flows toward the sea or a lake.
4 A small river
5 Where the river reaches the sea.
8 The starting point of a river, often on a mountain or hill.
9 Condensed water vapour falling from clouds.
10 The course along which the river runs.

Teachers' notes This worksheet needs to be used in conjunction with Worksheet 3, which shows the crossword for completion.

Rivers — Worksheet 3

What special words about rivers do I know?

Name __Sophia__   Date __11/11/23__

Teachers' notes This worksheet needs to be used in conjunction with worksheet 2, which lists the clues to solve the crossword.

Rivers Worksheet 4

What do I know about my local river?

Name _____ **Date** _____

Find out some information about your local river. You could use a map or the internet to help. The questions below will give you some ideas but you may be able to find out more information.

What is the nearest river to your school?
Where is its source?
Where does it flow to?
What are different sections of the river like?
Does it flood?
Does it carry traffic?
Do any important bridges cross it?

_____
_____
_____
_____
_____
_____

Teachers' notes If possible you could arrange a visit to your local river (after taking account of risk assessments). Some pupils will be able to find more information about the river than the questions suggest.

Rivers Worksheet 5

Can I describe the water cycle?

Name _____ Date _____

What is the water cycle? Can you describe it? Why is it called a 'cycle'? Look at the diagram and fill in each stage of the cycle. Then write your explanation below it.

Teachers' notes Higher ability pupils may have already completed this activity in Year 5 but it is useful revision for pupils of all abilities. The children may need to be reminded of the process: water evaporates from the surface of the sea (and from ground where rain has already fallen); the water vapour rises and forms clouds; as the clouds rise, and this happens particularly where they move over land, the water condenses to form droplets; the droplets gather together to make raindrops, which are heavy enough to fall; the rain falls on the land; water collects together in streams and rivers; the rivers flow to the sea.

Andrew Brodie: Geography Today 10–11 © A & C Black 2008

Rivers Worksheet 6

Why did early settlers choose to live by rivers?

Name _____ Date _____

Rivers have always been an important factor in human life. Many of the very first settlers would make their homes by a river and these places are where villages towns and cities developed. Can you think why the settlers would have chosen to live by rivers?

Look at the picture below and write an explanation for each activity you can see.

Teachers' notes This worksheet encourages the pupils to gain awareness of the importance of rivers for human activities. The children may need some support in identifying the six activities that would have been important to the settlers and in writing about them: fishing, travelling in a simple boat, washing themselves, washing clothing, growing crops on the fertile flood plain, using water for drinking and cooking.

Rivers Worksheet 7

Why did early settlers choose to live by rivers?

Name _____ Date _____

Rivers have always been an important factor in human life.

Many of the very first settlers would make their homes by a river and these places are where villages towns and cities developed. Look at the picture below and write down all the reasons that the people in the picture would have chosen to live by the river.

_____
_____
_____
_____
_____
_____
_____
_____
_____
_____

Teachers' notes The children should write about the six activities shown in the picture that would have been important to early settlers: fishing, travelling in a simple boat, washing themselves, washing clothing, growing crops on the fertile flood plain, using water for drinking and cooking.

Rivers Worksheet 8

What can I discover about a famous river?

Name _____ Date _____

Here are the names of some famous rivers in the world.

Nile	**Amazon**	**Mississippi**	**Danube**	**Rhine**
Zambezi	**Murray**	**Yellow**	**Yangtze**	**Niagara**

Choose one of the rivers and try to find out as much as you can about it.
The questions will give you some ideas but you may find lots more information.
You may be able to find maps and photographs so that you can create a presentation to share with your class. You may like to include your own sketch map of the route of the river.

How long is the river?
How does it compare to other rivers?
Does it have any special features?
What countries does it flow through?
What continent is it in?
Where does it flow into the sea?
Into which sea does it flow?
Where is its source?
What is the weather like where this river flows?

Teachers' notes This extension activity is open-ended and provides individuals, pairs or small groups the opportunity to complete some research in Atlases, maps and on the computer.

Andrew Brodie: Geography Today 10–11 © A & C Black 2008

Rivers — Vocabulary sheet 1

water cycle	rainfall	source
spring	stream	river
tributary	erosion	deposition
hill	slope	mountain
waterfall	valley	channel
mouth	litter	pollution
floodplain	meander	

MOUNTAINS

Contents

This unit is centred around the speaking and listening activity promoted by the CD-ROM presentation. This presentation shows mountains in the United Kingdom, Iceland, Central America, Africa, South America and eastern Europe. Pupils are encouraged to observe carefully, identifying features of mountain environments and of human activity within these. The two worksheets provide opportunities for individuals or pairs to carry out their own investigations using the internet or other resources, then to present their findings to the class. At the end of this unit there is an extension activity for pupils to use the skills and knowledge they have acquired throughout the *Geography Today* series.

This unit features:
- CD-ROM: MOUNTAINS 1–20
- Worksheets 1–2
- Vocabulary sheets 1–2
- Extension activity

Useful resources

- map of the local area
- world map and globe

Learning objectives

- asking geographical questions
- using appropriate geographical vocabulary
- collecting and recording evidence
- analysing evidence and drawing conclusions
- communicating in ways appropriate to the task and audience
- using secondary sources of information
- using ICT to help in geographical investigations
- drawing plans and maps at a range of scales
- using decision-making skills
- identifying and describing what places are like
- locating places and environments
- identifying how and why places change and how they may change in the future
- recognising physical and human features in the environment
- recognising how people can improve the environment or damage it, and how decisions about places and environments affect the future quality of people's lives
- identifying the physical features of rivers
- studying an environmental issue

The worksheets

Worksheet 1: The highest mountains in the United Kingdom
Worksheet 2: What can I discover about a famous mountain or mountain range?

The vocabulary sheets

The vocabulary sheets can be photocopied then made into flashcards, which can be used for both geography and literacy. It is helpful to read through the vocabulary with the pupils ensuring that they understand what each word means and why it is relevant to this subject. Pupils could sort the words into groups: countries, mountain ranges, volcano vocabulary, etc. They may also be able to add some words to the lists – you could set up a geography vocabulary board on the wall to which pupils could add words that they find.

The CD-ROM

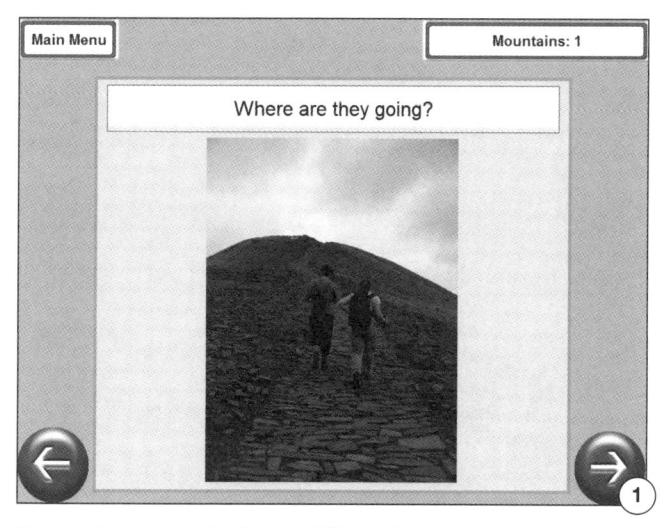

Mountains: 1 — *Where are they going?*

Discuss the photograph with the children. *Where could the people be going? Why are they going there? What are they walking on? Why is the path there? Why do they have boots and poles?*

The actual answers to the questions are as follows. *The two people are climbing a mountain called Pen y Fan in the Brecon Beacons in south Wales. They are tourists and therefore are going there to enjoy the view and to gain the exercise. They are walking on a well-worn path – it has been created especially for tourists. The people are wearing boots and carrying poles as they have come well prepared for the dangers of a mountain environment.* You could discuss with the children what these dangers might be.

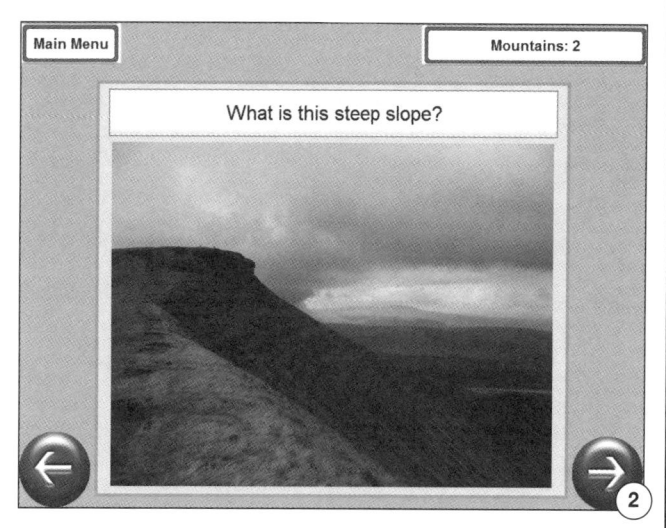

Mountains: 2 — *What is this steep slope?*

This photograph also shows Pen y Fan in the Brecon Beacons. The steep slope is called an escarpment or scarp face. Again, a well-worn path can be seen – does the creation of the path damage the mountain environment? The summit of Pen y Fan is 886 metres above sea level, which makes it a mountain rather than a hill. Definitions of what constitutes a mountain vary but one definition is that it must be over 600 metres above sea level.

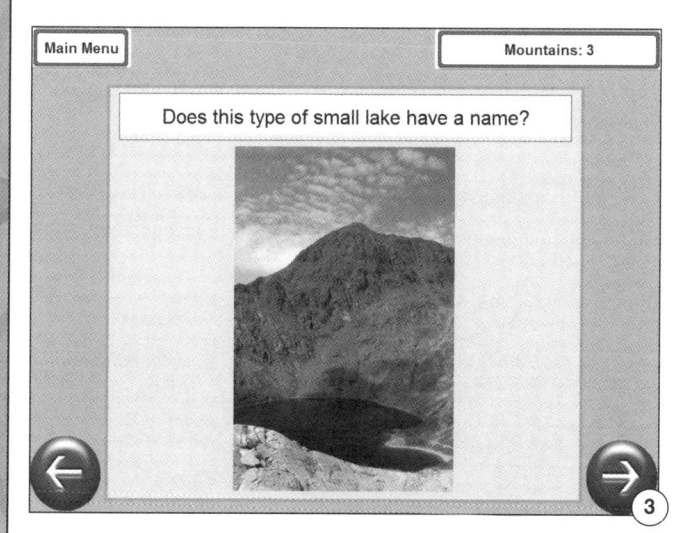

Mountains: 3 — *Does this type of small lake have a name?*

This small lake is high on a mountain in Snowdonia, north Wales. It is called a tarn or a corrie loch and forms in a dip called a cwm (pronounced coom) or corrie that has been created by glaciation. Encourage the pupils to look at other features of the photograph, including the steep slopes and the pathways. *Snowdon is the highest mountain in Wales with a height of 1085 m above sea level.* Can the pupils find the Brecon Beacons and Snowdonia on a map?

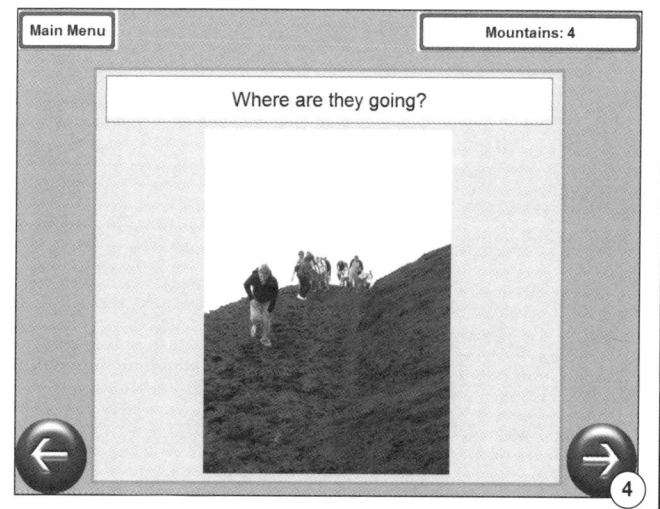

Mountains: 4 — *Where are they going?*

Can the pupils describe the scene? What do they notice about the background? Why is there no view behind the people? What do they notice about the ground? Is this in Wales like the previous photographs? Encourage the pupils to realise that the background is obscured by mist or smoke. The ground has no vegetation growing on it and looks muddy but, if the children look closely at the people's shoes and clothes, they will see that the ground is dry. The photograph was taken in Guatemala in Central America and the next slides will give clues regarding the special nature of the mountain.

The CD-ROM continued

Mountains: 5 — Where is he standing?

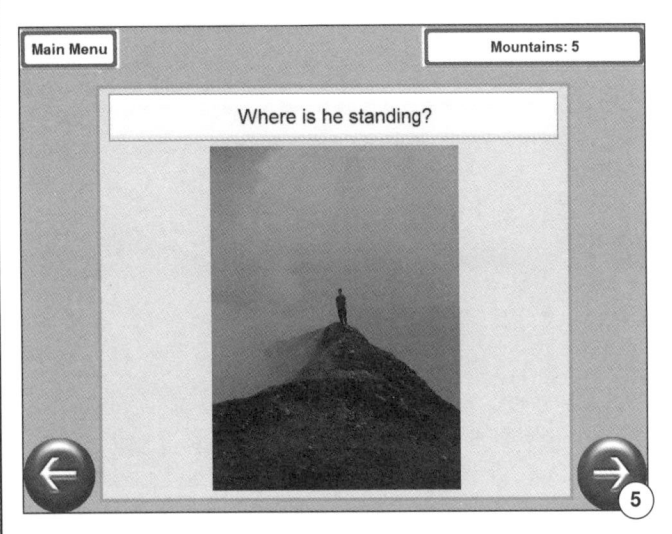

Discuss whether this looks like a safe place to stand. This photograph shows the summit of the special mountain that the tourists were climbing in the previous photographs. Have the pupils worked out why this mountain is special? Can the pupils find Guatemala on a world map or a globe?

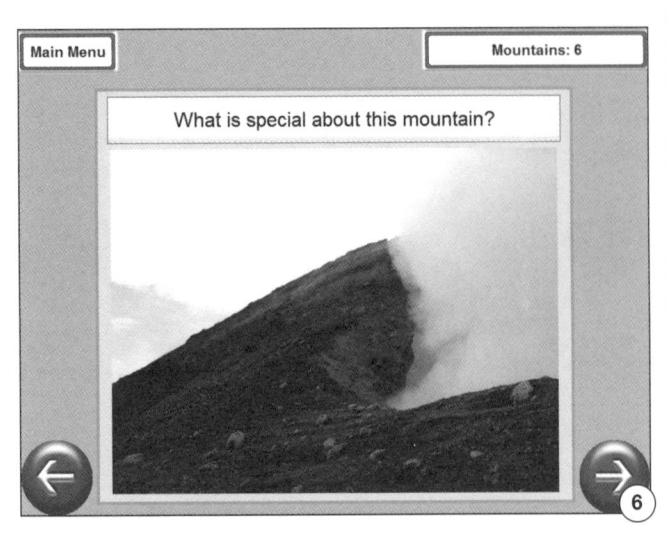

Mountains: 6 — What is special about this mountain?

Here the pupils can see that smoke is coming out of the top of the mountain so they have probably worked out that it is a volcano. Ask some children to look up 'volcano' in a dictionary, encyclopaedia or internet and to present their findings to the class.

Mountains: 7 — Would you go down there?

Pupils may be able to see that some people have climbed into the crater and have written some graffiti. Can pupils give reasons why they should not do that?

Explain to the pupils that this volcano is called the Volcan de Feugo and it is close to the city of Antigua (not to be confused with the Caribbean island) in Guatemala. Volcan de Feugo means 'volcano of fire' and is called this because it is constantly smoking. It rarely erupts violently. This mountain is 3763 metres high — pupils can compare this figure to the heights of Pen y Fan and Snowdon.

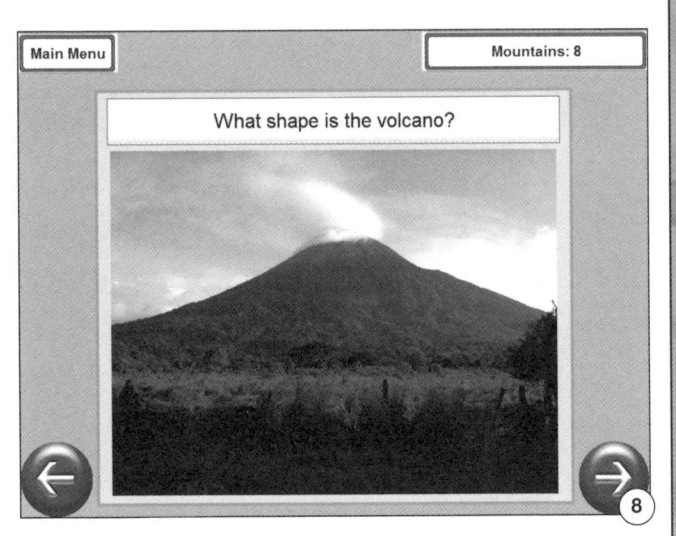

Mountains: 8 — What shape is the volcano?

The pupils may be able to describe the shape as a cone, the most usual shape for a volcano. This again is the constantly smoking Volcan de Feugo, which did erupt in 2007 causing molten lava to flow down the mountain. Other volcanos lie dormant for years then erupt suddenly causing great damage to the surrounding area.

The CD-ROM continued

Pupils will be able to identify this as a volcano because of the cone shape. This volcano is in Iceland. Iceland has many active volcanoes. One of the best known forms the island of Surtsey, off the south coast of the country. Surtsey did not exist as an island until 1963 when the volcano erupted under the sea. The eruptions continued for four years and an island of nearly three square kilometres was formed. Erosion by the Atlantic waves has caused much of the island to wash away and it is now about half the size that it was at its maximum. *This serves as a useful lesson to the children that the earth's surface is constantly changing, whether in the form of gradual river erosion or in the dramatic form of volcanoes or earthquakes. Can the pupils find Iceland on the world map or globe?*

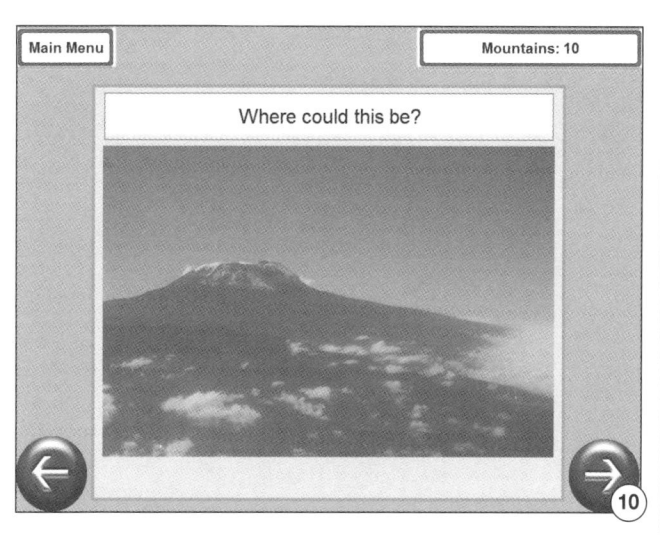

It is nearly impossible for pupils to guess where this is but you may like to play 'twenty questions' for pupils to find its location – it is Kilimanjaro in Tanzania, East Africa. Again, the shape as seen here is the shape of a volcano and Kilimanjaro has three volcanic cones but all are inactive. The highest peak is Uhuru Peak at 5895 metres. *Can the pupils find Kilimanjaro on the map?*

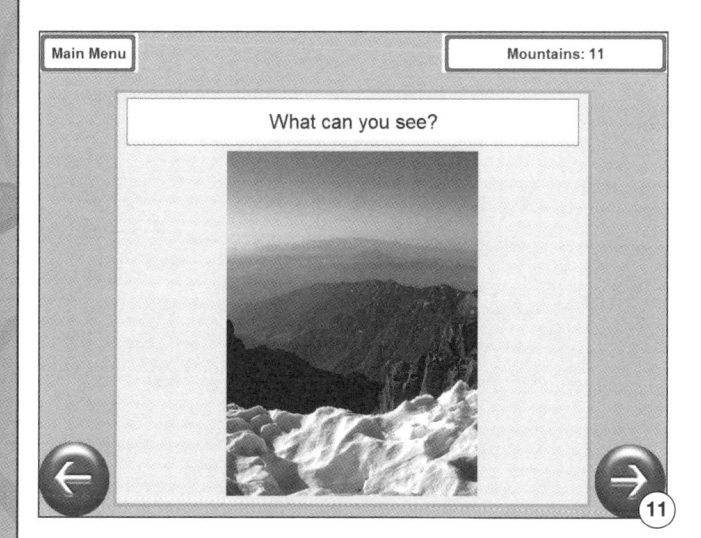

This mountain range is also in Africa – the range is called the Atlas Mountains. This photograph was taken in Morocco, North Africa, where the Atlas Mountains lie between the Sahara Desert and the coast. The snow is clearly visible as are many mountains extending into the distance. The Atlas Mountain range is 2400 kilometres long and the highest peak is 4167 metres above sea level.

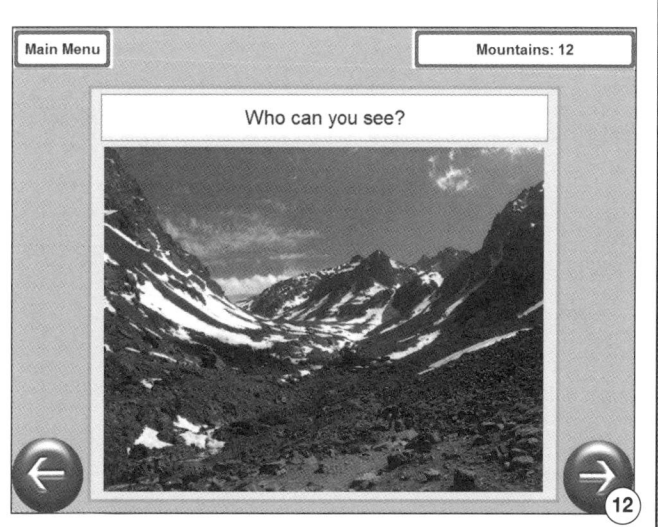

Even high in the Atlas Mountains there are tourists! Ask the children: *What are tourists?* They may be able to identify 'tourists' as people on holiday. Discuss what types of holiday the children have – do they ever explore areas? Explain the importance of safety: *Tourists must be prepared for dangers in the mountains, even in this country. Tourists should also consider the safety of the environment that they are visiting, taking care not to do damage to the landscape or the wildlife.*

The CD-ROM continued

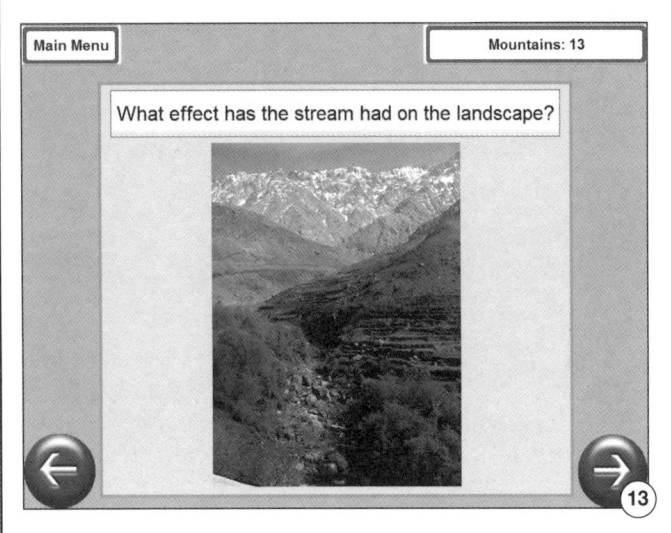

Mountains: 13 — What effect has the stream had on the landscape?

Here the stream has eroded its route through a valley in the Atlas Mountains – the v shape of the valley is clearly visible in both the foreground and the background. Pupils may also notice the greenery at this point in the landscape – grass and trees are growing here but the height at which trees will no longer grow is called the timberline. The children will also see the snow which has fallen above the snowline – the level above which the snow never melts completely.

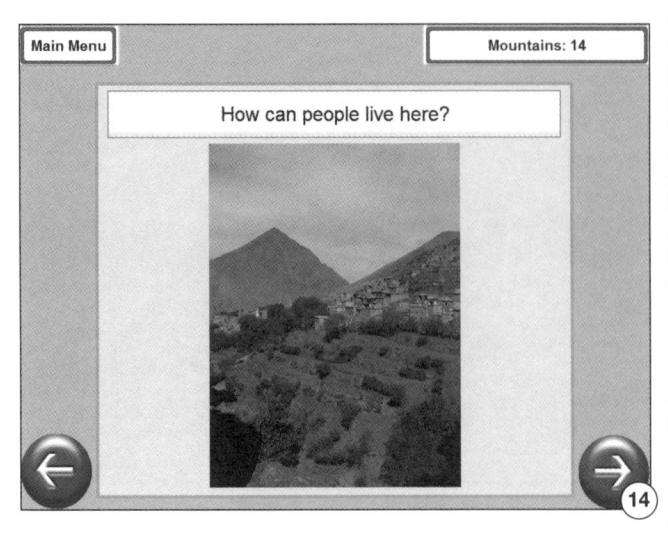

Mountains: 14 — How can people live here?

The landscape of the Atlas Mountains is harsh but provides the necessities for living, including water from the snowfields running in streams down the valleys. People are able to build houses from stone and, below the timberline, construct terraces for farming.

Can the children find the Atlas Mountains on a world map or globe?

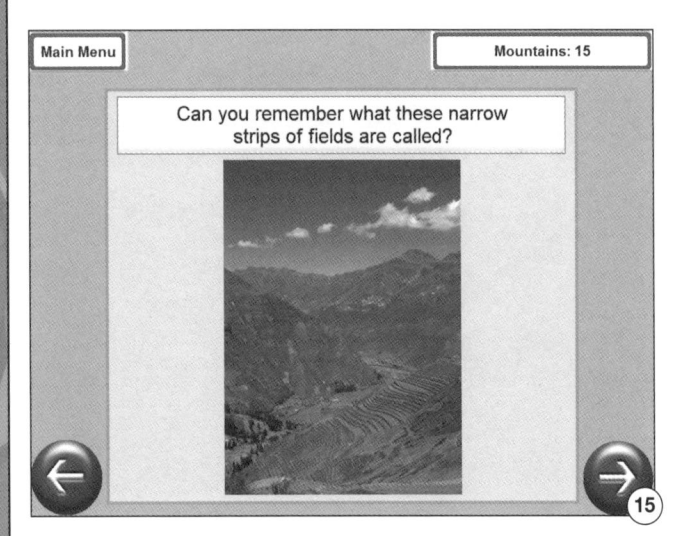

Mountains: 15 — Can you remember what these narrow strips of fields are called?

The children may remember the name 'terraces' from the last slide. Do they remember where the mountains on the last four slides were? This photograph is in a different continent – it shows the Andes Mountains in Peru. Looking closely pupils will observe the terraces on the slope but also the fields in the flat base of the valley. *Why is the base of the valley flat? This shows that a glacier has passed through the valley. A glacier consists of hard-packed ice that moves slowly down a valley causing erosion.*

Mountains: 16 — Who might visit this shop?

This photograph, taken in Peru in the Andes, shows a stall laid out for visiting tourists. The mountain range of the Andes extends for over 7000 kilometres along the west coast of South America. In some places it is 500 kilometres wide. The highest peak in the range is Aconcagua in Argentina with a height of 6962 metres.

The CD-ROM continued

Mountains: 17 — What can you see?

Encourage the pupils to describe what they can see – mountains covered in clouds, a peak and a ridge and, of course, the remains of buildings in the foreground. *This is Machu Picchu, a town that was built in about the year 1450 and which was abandoned approximately one hundred years later when the Spanish invaded South America, although the invaders never found it. Machu Picchu is built at a height of 2400 metres above sea level and is now a popular destination for tourists.* Can the children find Machu Picchu on a map or in an atlas?

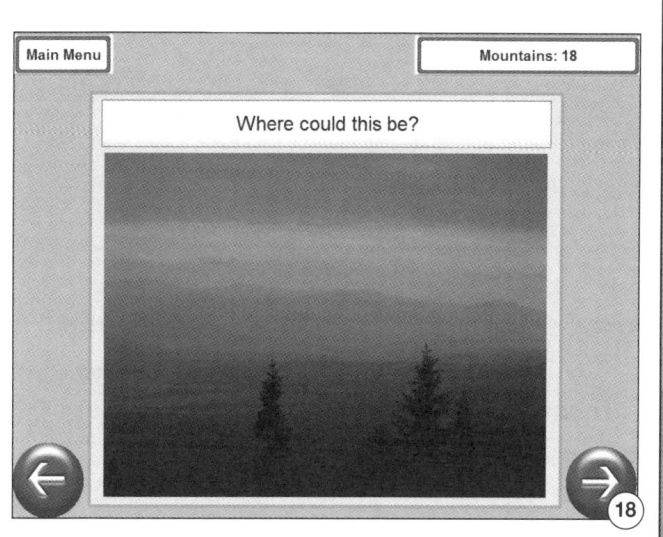

Mountains: 18 — Where could this be?

Ask the children to play 'twenty questions', where they are allowed to ask a question but will only have a 'yes' or 'no' answer. The final answer you are looking for is eastern Europe – this range of mountains is called the High Tatras and is situated in Slovakia, on the border with Poland.

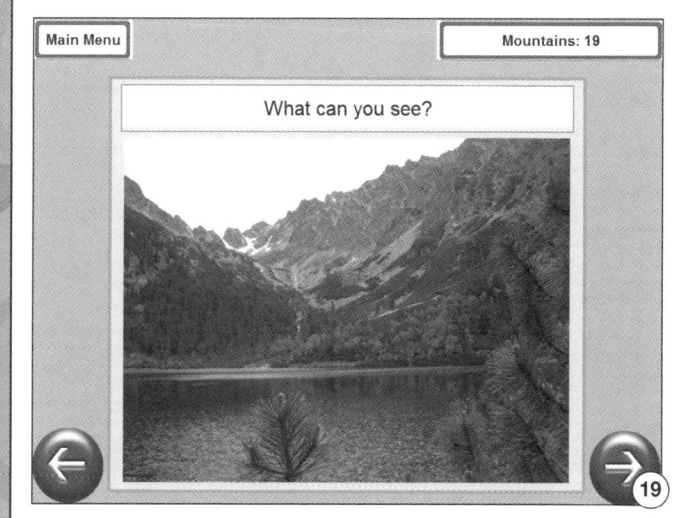

Mountains: 19 — What can you see?

Encourage the children to describe what they can see – a lake, a ridge of mountains, trees up to the timberline, a stream cascading down the mountain into the lake. *This photograph shows a lake in the High Tatra Mountains of Slovakia. Wildlife in the area includes bears, lynxes and wolves. The highest peak in the range has a height of 2655 metres.*

Mountains: 20 — Do you remember what this type of lake is called?

Pupils may remember that this is a tarn formed in a cwm or corrie. *This photograph again shows part of the High Tatras range in Slovakia, eastern Europe.* Can the children find the mountains on a map?

Mountains | Worksheet 1

The highest mountains in the United Kingdom

Name _____ Date _____

Using the internet, find out the names and heights of the highest mountain in Northern Ireland, Wales, Scotland and England. What else can you find out about each one?

Northern Ireland _____
_____
_____
_____

Wales _____
_____
_____
_____

Scotland _____
_____
_____
_____

England _____
_____
_____
_____

Teachers' notes Encourage the children to find out as much as possible about each mountain. What is its name and height? What mountain range is it in? What county is it in? How far is it from your school? You may wish to photocopy worksheet 7 from the Maps unit to ask the children to show the location of each of the four mountains and to give the appropriate map references.

Mountains | **Worksheet 2**

What can I discover about a famous mountain or mountain range?

Name _____ Date _____

Here are the names of some famous mountains or mountain ranges in the world.

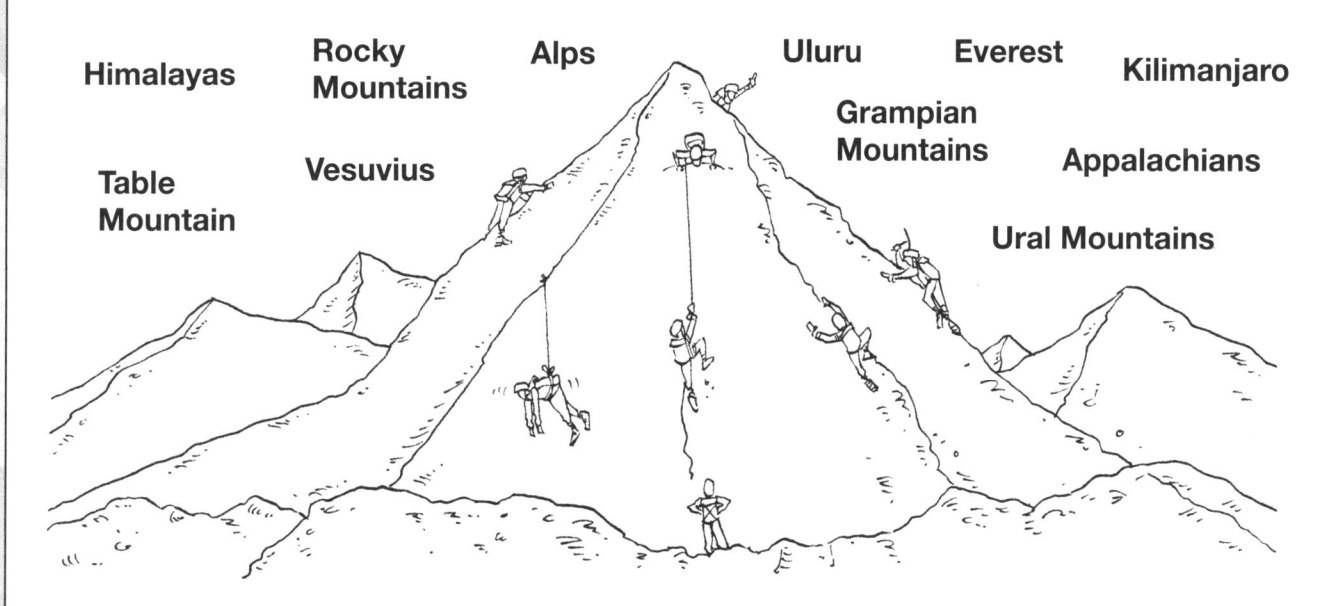

- Himalayas
- Rocky Mountains
- Alps
- Uluru
- Everest
- Kilimanjaro
- Grampian Mountains
- Appalachians
- Table Mountain
- Vesuvius
- Ural Mountains

Choose one of the above mountains or mountain ranges, or another mountain of your own choice, and try to find out as much as you can about it. The questions below will give you some ideas but you may find lots more information. You may be able to find maps and photographs so that you can create a presentation to share with your class. You may like to include your own sketch map of the location of the mountain.

- How high is the mountain or the tallest mountain in the range?
- What country or countries is it in?
- What continent is it in?
- Does it have any special features?
- What is the landscape like?
- What wildlife can be found in the area?
- What do people do in the area?
- Do tourists visit the area?
- What is the weather like in the area?

Teachers' notes This extension activity is open-ended and provides individuals, pairs or small groups the opportunity to complete some research in atlases, maps and on the computer.

Mountains — Vocabulary sheet 1

mountain	volcano	tourism
erosion	climate	atlas
Andes	High Tatras	Kilimanjaro
Tanzania	Guatemala	Slovakia
Morocco	Aconcagua	Argentina
Machu Picchu	Peru	Volcan de Fuego
Brecon Beacons	Pen y fan	Snowdon

Mountains — Vocabulary sheet 2

weather	valley	summit
blizzard	avalanche	snowstorm
snowdrift	snowline	tree line
timberline	landscape	snowfield
terrace	escarpment	scarp face
cwm	tarn	peak
eruption	active	inactive

EXTENSION ACTIVITY

Name _____

Choose any country in the world to investigate. Present your findings to the rest of the class.

Here are some ideas that you could research, though you may also have ideas of your own:

- What is the name of the country?
- In which continent is it situated?
- Is it on the coast or inland?
- If it is on the coast, what sea or seas is it adjacent to?
- What other countries border this one?
- How big is the country?
- What is its population?
- What language do the people speak?
- What currency is used?
- Do any famous people come from that country?
- Is the country famous for any particular sports?
- Does the country have any famous buildings? Is the country famous for anything else?
- What mountains, if any, does the country have?
- What rivers?
- Are there any special physical features?

Once you have found answers to some of these questions you could create a written presentation about your chosen country. You could illustrate your presentation with photographs and maps.

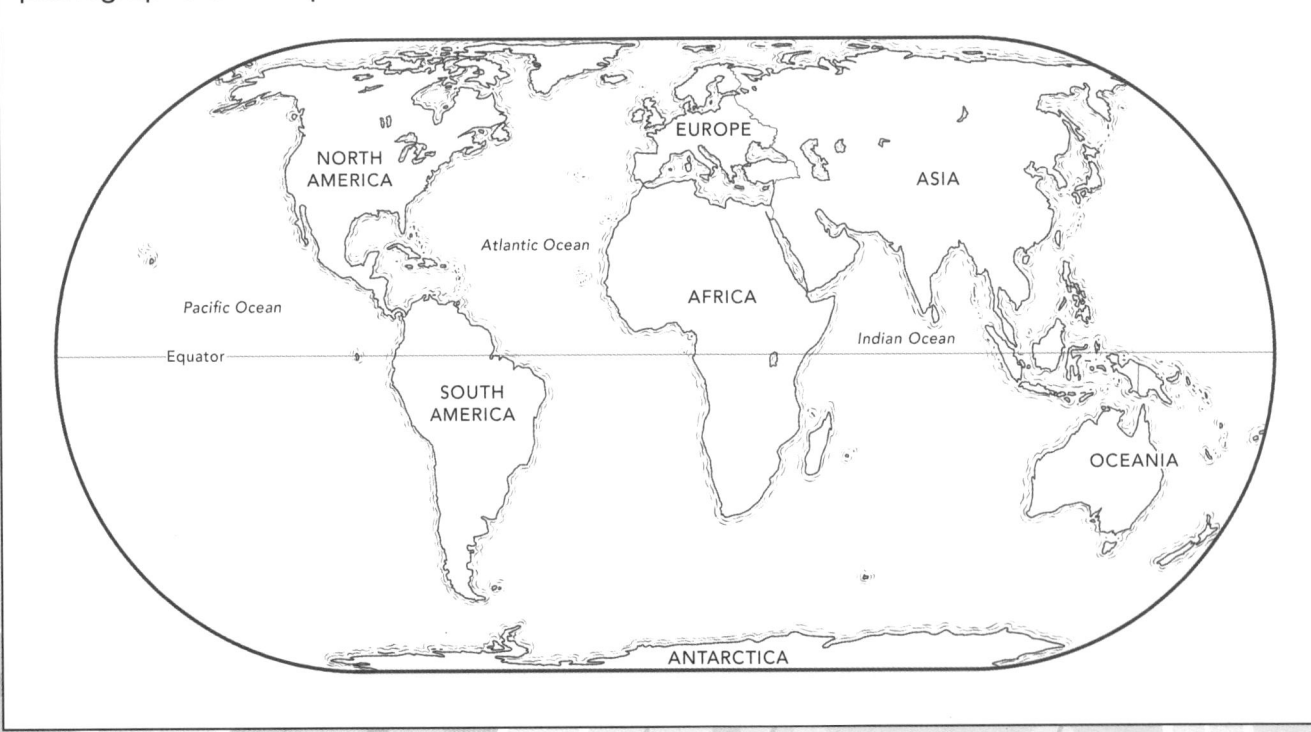

Teachers' notes This final activity in the book provides pupils with the opportunity to research a country of their choice applying some of their geographical skills and knowledge. Pupils could work in pairs, groups or individually. You may wish to suggest a specific format for their presentations so that you could create a class encyclopedic atlas in the form of a book or computer presentation.